Of Mud & Lotuses

Of Mud & Lotuses

DREAMING THE LIVES OF BUDDHIST WOMEN

PAULA ARAI

Foreword by KARMA LEKSHE TSOMO

SHAMBHALA

Shambhala Publications, Inc.
2129 13th Street
Boulder, Colorado 80302
www.shambhala.com

Cover art: lumyaisweet - stock.adobe.com
Cover & interior design: Kate E. White

9 8 7 6 5 4 3 2 1

First Edition
Printed in the United States of America

Shambhala Publications makes every effort to print on acid-free, recycled paper.
Shambhala Publications is distributed worldwide by Penguin Random House, Inc., and its subsidiaries.

LIBRARY OF CONGRESS CATALOGING-IN-PUBLICATION DATA
Names: Arai, Paula Kane Robinson, author | Karma Lekshe Tsomo, 1944– other
Title: Of mud and lotuses: dreaming the lives of Buddhist women / Paula Arai, Karma Lekshe Tsomo.
Description: Boulder: Shambhala Publications, 2026. | Includes bibliographical references. |
Identifiers: LCCN 2025041794 | ISBN 978-1-64547-521-7 trade paperback
Subjects: LCSH: Women—Religious aspects—Buddhism | Buddhist nuns—Religious life | Religious life—Buddhism | Monastic and religious life (Zen Buddhism)—China
Classification: LCC BQ4570.W6 A73 2026 | DDC 294.3082—dc23/eng/20260114
LC record available at https://lccn.loc.gov/2025041794

The authorized representative in the EU for product safety and compliance is eucomply OÜ, Pärnu mnt 139b-14, 11317 Tallinn, Estonia, hello@eucompliancepartner.com.

May all beings be nourished and liberated in
the womb of wisdom and compassion.

In the spring of the thirty-first year of the Hongwu reign period [1398], on the first day of the First Month, I lit some incense and sat quietly inside my chambers. I was perusing some ancient sutras and classics, my mind and spirit focused and settled, when suddenly a purplish-gold radiance completely filled every corner of my room. Indistinctly, as if I were asleep and dreaming, I saw the Bodhisattva Guanyin appear from within the radiance in the form of the Great Compassionate One. Standing on her thousand-petaled jeweled lotus, she held in her hand a rosary made of the seven precious gems. She moved in front of me, and before I knew it, I was riding a kingfisher blue cloud vehicle, above which there opened a five-colored jeweled canopy, an array of pearly banners and precious flags inviting us to come forward. Flapping and fluttering, they waved over the distance without seeming to be rooted anywhere at all.

From the preface by Empress Xu (1361–1407)
to *The Rarest Sutra of Great Merit Spoken by the Buddha and Received by the Empress Humane and Filial of the Great Ming in a Dream*[1]

CONTENTS

FOREWORD

In the future, when the story of Buddhism is told, perhaps the most striking features will be the international shifts in gender perspectives that empowered women in Buddhist societies around the world toward the end of the twentieth century.

In this volume, the creative collection of stories about women in diverse Buddhist texts, histories, and cultures guides the reader on a journey of what was and what might have been. Arai highlights women's power and disenfranchisement with equal insight. Lyrically, she invites us to stretch our imagination and our empathy to include the millions of women throughout the ages who have encountered the Buddha's teachings and meaningfully incorporated them in their families, communities, and personal development—often unnoticed.

Of Mud and Lotuses is a groundbreaking statement of a new vision emerging from the efforts of millions of women, over centuries and expressly in the last fifty years, who have worked for gender equality in Buddhist societies—notably full ordination for female monastics. Arai presents a kaleidoscope of Buddhist women's experiences with artistry and in clear violation of the patriarchal boundaries that have thus far defined and constricted Buddhist scholarship, ethics, and authority. Her work unfurls an entirely new category that honors human emotions and matriarchal perspectives, bursting through all patriarchal confines of intellectual acceptability. Directly attending to the affective dimension of human experience, the multiple perspectives that emerge from the narratives highlight women's emotional intelligence, raising storytelling to a fine art.

Throughout the book, Arai challenges preconceptions about the female body that, for centuries, have tainted the Buddhist teachings. Even when the third noble truth affirms the liberative power of the teachings for all, a female body has been commonly viewed as a defective vehicle for achieving liberation. As a consequence, women have often eschewed institutional power and turned to contemplative and ritual practices, manifesting Buddhist values in everyday life. Through the stories of Mahaprajapati, Shrimala, and others, philosophical concepts come to life in practical ways. Inspired by Buddhist texts and teachings, virtue and compassion have come to naturally, meaningfully imbue the everyday lives of the fortunate in distinct ways across generations. How fascinating to learn how the teachings have resonated, both very similarly and very differently, among women of diverse time periods and cultures.

Framed in narrative style with commentary, Arai engages in creative thought experiments to foreground acts of resistance and resilience. For example, she highlights the earnest, day-to-day practices of centuries of women who offer alms to monastics as a key Dharma practice—not as scullery maids confined to the kitchen, but as sincere embodiments of generosity, a key Buddhist principle. She also notes that the Buddhist traditions have continually transformed over the centuries, sometimes expanding in inclusive ways. For example, the teaching that all sentient beings have Buddha-nature, which became prominent more than five centuries after the Buddha, are inspiring for anyone who has ever questioned their worth or their potential to navigate this dusty world.

Arai does not shy away from critical, often controversial issues. For instance, she questions whether young monks may develop pride or arrogance, not to mention gender bias, from the first *Garudharma* practice that requires even the most senior nuns to rise and pay respect to brand-new monks. In a radical move, Arai flips the ancient script that perpetuates preconceptions about the defects of a female rebirth. To balance textual references to the shortcomings of a female body, she lists the parallel shortcomings of a male body.

Navigating waves of culture, the stories open a window onto the resilience and compassion of remarkable women over a wide swath of Buddhist history, from fifth-century-B.C.E. India to contemporary North America. We read the story of a fifteenth-century Japanese woman who secretly, reverently smuggled her hair inside a statue she donated to a male-only monastery. Other women similarly challenged the taboos surrounding women's allegedly polluted bodies by creating sacred images out of their own hair. These transgressive practices shatter presumptions about the submissive, acquiescent Asian woman. The stories from eighteenth-century Japan vividly bring the reader in touch with the dangers and fears that attend the birthing of children, realities that most women face even today. Another important insight is the startlingly powerful effect of family connections, especially the close relationships between successive generations of women—daughters, mothers, grandmothers—that may be absent among contemporary Dharma practitioners. Creating fictionalized stories to fill the gaps in Buddhist women's history vividly brings the ingenuity and values of these ordinary and extraordinary women to life.

This guided tour through different eras of Buddhist history imagines innovative expressions of Buddhist practice over time through the eyes and life situations of women of different generations and social standings, sparking new insights and raising many questions. Learning about the everyday experiences of Buddhist women stretches our imagination and opens windows into cultures beyond our own. Introducing figures who were poets, mystics, royalty, teachers, and often leading proponents of Buddhism disrupts common preconceptions of Buddhist women as boring, marginal, or repressed. Stretching beyond history, this poetic and intellectually profound work breaks through the pervasive binary assumption that one's heart and mind are two.

Karma Lekshe Tsomo
Cofounder and past president, Sakyadhita
International Association of Buddhist Women
Professor Emerita, University of San Diego

ACKNOWLEDGMENTS

The stories of all the people, living and dead, who contributed to this book—those who informed, modeled, corrected, challenged, inspired, affirmed, encouraged, and supported me—are worthy of their own books, books whose pages would be filled with anecdotes from stimulating conversations, lightning bolts of insight, humility, laughter, awe, and, most of all, gratitude.

The living women who shared their Dharma journeys to help others grow and learn manifested mountainous courage and oceanic generosity. Their stories are filled with the visceral realities of navigating situations that are unfortunately not uncommon in our *Saha* world of suffering. I humbly bow my head to their resilience, creativity, and wisdom.

The historical women who animate the pages of this book came to life for me through the expertise of numerous scholars and researchers. Each of these scholars has rich and deep stories about how they developed their insights and understanding, traversing the globe to dwell in libraries, archives, and temples. Through their published materials and personal communications, the world of Buddhist women expanded in my mind in unanticipated ways. They helped me see that the history of Buddhist women is more amazing than what I had imagined.

The illustrious erudition of Dr. Beata Grant and Dr. Ronald Egan supported me with crucial guidance and knowledge regarding Chinese Buddhist women. Dr. Lori Meeks's impeccable research illuminated significant aspects of Japanese Buddhist women's contributions and activities. Dr. Kevin Trainor, Venerable Dr. Mahinda Deegalle, and Carolyn Dille provided critical and specific information that opened me up to the world of early Sri Lankan Buddhism. Dr. Steve Jenkins shared gems of knowledge about the Indian Buddhist tradition. Dr. Eun-su Cho distilled the history of Korean Buddhist women into a list of representatives to include in the ritual. To each of you, I offer nine bows of gratitude.

The Frederick P. Lenz Foundation for American Buddhism's contribution to this volume is a story of visionary generosity, notably focused on supporting Buddhist women. I am grateful for their grant, which facilitated the publication of this book. For more information about the foundation, visit www.fredericklenz-foundation.org.

The journey of bringing this book to fruition wove through numerous communities of deep-hearted people, each offering helpful feedback, affirmations, and living energy. Reflecting on each of the communities that invited me in, a multilayered intertwined story comes into view. Even as each community has its own dynamics and concerns, a common thread weaves us together in a commitment to justice, especially regarding Buddhist women, and for many, explicitly engaging the world with wisdom and compassion. For your contributions to this ongoing story, I'd like to thank you all: Union Theological Seminary, Graduate Theological Union's Women's Studies in Religion, Jodo Shinshu Center for Buddhist Education, Federation of Dharma School Teachers, Federation of Buddhist Women's Associations, San Mateo Buddhist Temple, San Francisco Zen Center, Upaya Zen Center, Ancient Dragon Gate Zen Center, Ocean Gate Zen Center, Brooklyn Zen Center, and attendees at our Watershed Center retreat that celebrated the ritual and healing ways of Buddhist women.

Undergirding this book of stories are the insightful, editorial eagle eyes of Dr. Stephanie Kaza and Peter Schumacher. Out of pure generosity, Stephanie offered me a scholarly gift worth more than gold. She offered extremely helpful wisdom during the early stages of writing and then did a thorough review of the manuscript: numerous single-spaced pages filled with astute suggestions and discerning comments. After tending to those ministrations, Peter Schumacher, my editor at Shambhala, applied his perceptive expertise to make the book clearer and more accessible, helping me find hidden depths in the stories.

Numerous stories involving a dedicated group of people culminated in the ritual in the epilogue, "Homage to Our Buddhist Mothers." A public enactment of this ritual launched the 2024 Soto Zen Buddhist Association's year of Celebrating the Voices of Women, which was cosponsored by the Institute of Buddhist Studies (IBS). I bow in honor to each person who expresses gratitude to the women, named and unnamed, who live Dharma. Your grateful heart is encoded in each enactment of the ritual, an ongoing story of women embodying Dharma.

The women who initiated the creation of the Eshinni and Kakushinni Professor of Women and Buddhist Studies chair at IBS and the continuing stream of donors are a visionary tale of determination and generosity. Women have been the lifeblood of the community since its founding in the thirteenth century, and women in the twenty-first century galvanized their effort to advance the formal graduate-level study of Buddhist women. I am profoundly grateful that my life has intersected with this story by being the first steward of this history-making academic chair, making my life a dream come true.

The story of IBS is itself an inspirational story, for it is an institution that rose out of the travails of Japanese Buddhist immigrants who ventured into a new land with a harmonizing vision and prevailed over the racist fearmongering that forced them into federal incarceration camps during World War II. Each person in this community holds a story in their heart that intersects with this history. Many are committed to offering our society another path—a path of justice and kindness honed by critical reasoning. A deep pool of gratitude stirs in me for the conducive environment generated by my colleagues at IBS, including the prior president Rev. Dr. David Matsumoto, the current president, Dr. Scott Mitchell, and members of the IBS Board of Trustees.

The people who make serious and complicated life choices to study at IBS, whether in Berkeley or online, fill me with hope. Invariably, the classes I am blessed to guide are filled with students who engage in transformative thinking. Such was the case with my course, "Buddhist Women's Liberating Power" held in the spring term of 2023. Together we mined the depths and soared the heights, inspiring me to write this book. A heartfelt and sincere bow of gratitude to Letesa Isler, Melissa Opel, Vincent Moore, and Amanda Karys. Students in my "Methods in Buddhist Studies" class were assigned an early draft of the manuscript as an example of what is illuminated in the Buddhist tradition through a narrative method. For their feedback and encouragement, I bow in gratitude. Thank you, Amy Shoemaker, Sumreen Chaudhry, Vonn Magnin, Igor Makasyuk, Victor Ogundipe, Dennis Sarni, and Scott Morgensen. An additional bow of gratitude for Scott's scintillating discussions about gender, a field in which he has a PhD and is a professor in his own right. Indeed, the stories of each of these seekers goes deep into the heart of our humanity, with me and this book two of their fortunate beneficiaries.

All daughters of the Buddha have nourished this book, and my gratitude flows deep into the past and swells far into the future. In this present time, I want to explicitly thank the cofounder of Sakyadhita (Daughters of the Buddha) International Association of Buddhist Women, Venerable Dr. Karma Lekshe Tsomo. Her leadership is a beacon in our times, instrumental in globally transforming Buddhist women. If I wrote her story, it would sound like an imagined ideal of how wisely and powerfully a woman can wield the Dharma in the service of ameliorating suffering. I offer you one long continuous bow of gratitude for all you do for me and our world.

Friends honed in the school of life, many, too, with advanced degrees—each with stories that would fill fascinating volumes of adventure, inspiration, perspicacity in the face of hardship, and creativity in addressing quandaries—there is no valley deep enough for me to bow in to fully express the profoundness of my gratitude for buoying me up along this meandering and precious path of life.

My story of Dr. Miranda Shaw would be titled *Kalyāṇamitra*. You taught me what it means to be a *kalyāṇamitra*, a companion with whom I can soar into subtle conversations about nuanced points of Buddhist philosophy, revel in new perspectives and areas of inquiry, and penetrate obstacles of heart and mind to open a path for lucid insights to emerge. A wizard of words, you have worked your magical ministrations on my writing, which will take me many lifetimes to repay. Would that I could entreat flowers to bloom out your window every morning so you could sense how grateful I am for the blossoms of wisdom and kindness you have bestowed on me for over forty years, connected through countless hours on the phone.

Kai, my treasured husband, thank you for all the daily gifts—keeping the hearth warm, healthy food served, garden flourishing, windows sparkling, errands run—each a gift that freed time to flow into these pages. Thank you for also training Aki. When walking in the woods, it is pure joy to behold the antics of a happy and sweet dog. Thank you, Aki, for staying by my side as I sit and type. You have perfected the virtue of patience. That our story, Kai, is unfolding from a classroom at Waseda University to blessed matrimony living in the embrace of redwoods, golden retriever bouncing around in our midst, is another dream come true.

Kenji, thank you for sharing this pilgrimage with me, an odyssey for the ages. Thank you for making me a mother in this life. I am sure you were my teacher in the past, for you continue to help me grow and learn. Without you as my son, there are many stories I would not have been able to tell, so many insights I would not have had about the power mothers must summon to raise a child. Indeed, it is thanks to you in my life that I know in my bones that without Buddhist women there would be no Buddhist tradition to pass along generation to generation.

To my parents, Masuko Arai Robinson and Lucian Ford Robinson, and my one-hundred-year-old Zen nun teacher, Kitō Shunkō, thank you for modeling how to blossom in the mud, a gift that illuminates beauty and nurtures love in all seasons.

Under the redwoods of the Santa Cruz Mountains,
Hands raised in respect, head bowed in gratitude,
Paula
July 15, 2025

Of Mud & Lotuses

OPENING

Wombs for Liberating Dharma

As mother and daughter approach the lush garden, the fragrance of jasmine blossoms wafts through the morning air. A peacock's cry announces their arrival to the sacred Indian Buddhist grounds. Clouds of incense floating from pots hanging from the trees beckon them to walk into the Sanchi compound. Moving first to the *Gandhakuṭi*, the perfumed chamber where the Buddha's presence lingers, they bow with palms together.[1] As they walk toward the stupa, the intricacy of carvings on its surface come into view.

"Oh, Mama, look at the beautiful carvings of women on the gate! That mound looks like the bump on your belly. I hope the baby is born soon so we can play together. I can't wait!"

"I'm excited for the baby, too. You know, dear one, my mother brought me here when I was about to give birth to you. And she was brought here by her mother before I was born. Each visit brought us a healthy baby, but not everyone is so fortunate. I am so grateful for the blessing of your health. You are growing into such an observant and caring girl. Your grandmother would be so happy if she could see the joy and curiosity in your eyes."

Hand in hand, they go to make offerings and pray for the blessings of a safe and healthy birth.

Women can imagine their bodies affirmed in the monument at the core of the Buddhist tradition: the stupa.[2] We can picture how the symbolism of the stupa as the womb of a Buddha might spark a conversation between a mother and daughter such as the one above. Intimate exchanges, however, are not commonly recorded and preserved, though they are vital to how women shared their wisdom over the millennia.

To hear Buddhist women's voices reverberating through our history and our hearts is liberating. Each voice we hear functions like a distillation of countless voices that we have not heard. Though materials about and by women have burgeoned in the last decades, it is still the case that most everything we hear about the Buddhist tradition is distorted due to the yawning holes in our knowledge of what the vast majority of Buddhist women thought, felt, and did. A more balanced view requires creative strategies to explore how Buddhist women experienced suffering and liberation in personal and communal contexts.

A guiding aim of this volume is to hear the voices of women and dispel the fog of misogyny that obscures our view of Dharma. In part 1, I present stories of women liberating Dharma from concepts and conditions that generate suffering for women. These stories integrate my Dharma-informed imagination with scholarship on historical figures, texts, and contexts. The stories in this section join the emerging field of creative histories.[3] Creative histories weave evidence-based historical events and texts with plausible characters and events. The aim of this genre is to envision the people whose voices and actions were not recorded. The numerous stories of powerful women I have encountered in my historical studies inspired me to elaborate on the available historical examples to provide vividly detailed stories of the many ways Buddhist women of the past have liberated themselves and others. To explore the possibilities of what might have happened for which we do not have evidence, I envision ways women in various times and places might have navigated misogynist texts, rules, and situations they may have faced. In doing so, my aim is to enrich the imagination of my readers and thereby empower them in their own spiritual journeys. In the introductions to each story, I delineate which parts of the story are evidence-based and which parts are fictive. In part 2, the stories draw on ethnographic material I gathered from deep conversations with several contemporary women. Listening to their stories reveals the continuing challenges, perspicacity, and resilience of women today. Taken together, the stories in this volume offer a journey into the lives of Buddhist women that spans twenty-five hundred years and extends across South Asia, East Asia, and North America.

I hope to inspire research and interpretations that are inclusive and empower women to wield Dharma in ways that are liberative. Writing liberating histories of women enables us to see the whole tradition more clearly, for without including women everything is distorted. The scholarly sources I have consulted and the fictive characters I have created suggest possibilities of where to look for information and what to recognize as knowledge. I aspire to generate options for living practitioners to wield Dharma in the face of oppressive conditions, injustices, and life challenges by including stories of living women who wield the liberating power of Dharma to face the suffering in their lives. Lastly, I want to empower people to create a world of less suffering and delusions, a world of more peace and love. Each dimension of these aims is integral to the larger interdependent nature where no one is fully liberated until all are liberated.

Setting out on this quest, I was inspired by the clarion voice of Buddhist scholar Miranda Shaw. She awakens us to a female-centered view of the early Buddhist landscape: The half dome shape of a stupa reflects a supine pregnant belly. Her paradigm-shifting insight opens wide a window onto how a woman might experience the central architectural form of the early Buddhist tradition. Shaw fills in the picture of a stupa mound with significant details and illuminating information. Designed to harbor

Shakyamuni Buddha's relics, a stupa is a womb for an enlightened being: "That the stupa is a womb is reflected in the Buddhist terminology. The mound is termed 'womb' (*garbha*), while the central receptacle encasing the relics is the 'egg' (*aṇḍa*)."[4] She directs attention to the fecund imagery of a stupa site, including vegetation, fruit trees, and "female figures whose ample breasts and hips proclaim their fertility."[5] Taking into account a fuller range of symbols and images, Shaw concludes that "the integrated body of imagery [around a stupa is] the visual vocabulary of a theology of female generative power."[6]

I imagined what the Buddhist world would feel like if that's the way I was raised to see it. The story with which I began this book was what I saw. I felt fully and completely affirmed and included just as I am: a daughter, a mother, and a follower of the Buddhist path. These insights of the fecundity built into a central early Buddhist monument summons us to open our minds to see from a woman's perspective, a perspective that promises to qualitatively deepen our understanding of the Buddhist tradition.

Although scholarship has made strides in recognizing the ways in which women have been limited by certain teachings, institutions, and practices, most of women's activities are obscured in the mists of time and clouded over by interpretations of history that are filtered through an elite male monastic perspective. The prevailing interpretation of institutionalized male practices and exclusionary doctrines obscure how women might have responded. A prominent and widely circulated narrative—reinforced by scholarly selectivity—leaves the impression that women were impaired in their effort to seek liberation from suffering. However, the negative treatment of women is not the only important part of the story.

We know that women have been active since the inception of the Buddhist tradition. Moreover, that all people come out of a woman's womb is an underappreciated fact in much of historical analysis and is often treated as if it were just a metaphor. The fact that without a woman the Buddhist tradition would not have been born is in some ways simplistic and other ways fundamental. Focusing on this fact can help us see how women have been practically, historically, and conceptually vital to the founding and development of this tradition.

Maya Devi nurtured the Buddha-to-be in her body. The foods she ate were the first food offerings. Mahaprajapati, the mother who raised him as her own, provided necessities that would eventually blossom into his awakening. His wife, Yashodhara, bequeathed more love, manifested in their son, Rahula, who would become part of the next generation to pass on Dharma his father taught.

Women actively nurtured in their bodies and fed from their breasts all those who followed the Buddha. Women's hands tended to each follower as they learned to walk and cared for them when they were sick. These women embodied the wisdom that compassion is a concrete act of care. In a stream flowing from days of yore, all the women who gave birth to these mothers made a critical contribution to what became the Buddhist tradition. In a current streaming onward, all the children who passed Dharma forward connect us to awakened wisdom that is integral to the Buddhist tradition. Women were successful in nurturing a tradition that now spans the world and for over twenty-five hundred years offered direction to those aching to stop suffering.

Nonetheless, the historical record of women's activities and contributions to the Buddhist tradition are incomplete, as the types of pragmatic and everyday activities in which women were engaged, such as those highlighted in the preceding paragraph, were not recorded. Moreover, a significant amount of the information we do have is filtered through ideas and assumptions that were developed without women's input in mind. Consequently, to dispel the distorted and often negative images we do have, we need to engage a multisensorial approach. Fortified by research and amplified by imagination, I have employed the creative expedient of storytelling to bring to life Buddhist women over the centuries who laughed and cried in ways that are continuous with our own. Encouraged by the knowledge that Buddhist sutras are replete with stories that animate the teachings—and that historical people crafted and recorded these stories—I realized it was still relevant and valuable to compose Dharma stories and decided to take it upon myself to do so. I can visualize women inspired and energized by the Buddhist teachings. I can imagine how women could live in accord with Dharma. I can see women navigating situations to ameliorate suffering. I can ponder ways women are likely to respond with compassion. I can engage in storytelling to make the concerns and contributions of women immediate.

I launch my effort not with the question—Did women seek the cessation of suffering?—but rather—How did women seek the cessation of suffering? Adding one word opens avenues of insight that regard women as agents in their own lives, as caring, hardworking, and serious. Exploring the cumulative tradition from the perspective of women's concerns will help us uncover visionary ways women might have integrated teachings on wisdom and loving-kindness into their lives.

Indeed, stories can help us see aspects and dynamics of the tradition not reflected in known records and materials. Through historically informed fictional storytelling, we can enrich our awareness of what was socially and culturally plausible for a woman trying to live according to Dharma. Stories can explore approaches women might have taken to live with unfair and repressive conditions. They can illuminate the view from the underside of repressive structures, teachings, and practices, which is often fuller than the view from above. Even when we do not know historical details, we can breathe life into Dharma teachings by imagining options that might alleviate suffering. It is harder to imagine how the Buddhist tradition would have flourished if women had not been creative and courageous in navigating the challenging and sometimes unjust conditions of their lives.

To imagine women in the fullness and intricacies of life, I ground my stories in particular contexts. Composing narratives based on substantial historical and ethnographic scholarship helps us envision how a woman shapes and is shaped by numerous conditions, including sociohistorical and cultural contexts and linguistic, economic, and political dynamics. Such stories animate religious teachings and concepts of gender employed by the person and community. They require interpreting how a woman might view the historical evidence recorded in texts, expressed in art and architecture, codified in rules, institutionalized in organizational structures, and encoded in ritual practices. Exploring how a person might respond to demeaning and oppressive dynamics by wielding their insights into the nature of delusion, desire, and aversion opens space to see women's activities and contributions.

In contrast to the prominent focus on male domination and misogyny—where significant Buddhist texts or practices present negativity toward women—I center my stories on liberating approaches women took, might have taken, or could take to live Dharma. Some stories focus on troubling sutras and practices, including nuns unilaterally bowing to monks and derogatory pronouncements about women's bodies being a constraint on attaining enlightenment. Other stories explore how women engaged with fundamental challenges in life by applying Dharma in basic yet unheralded ways, such as waking up extra early to prepare food to offer as alms, writing a letter to share wisdom, mentoring a young woman, or grieving a death. I chose a range of sociohistorical settings for my stories, from the earliest days of the tradition in India into Sri Lanka and China and through to twentieth-century Japan. Since learning how women lived Dharma in the past required some sleuthing and imagination to weave knowledge into stories, I benefited from experts' assessment of the plausibility of details regarding stories I placed outside of my deeper understanding of modern Japan.

To write the several nonfiction stories about women living on the West Coast of the United States, I had the benefit of being able to draw from in-depth conversations with them. Each of them shared from a place of honesty and vulnerability. In addition, I was able to ask these contemporary women questions for clarification, and they were able to assess and correct what I wrote.

Their living voices provide a view of contemporary contexts and concerns. The difficulties they live with and navigate demonstrate the ongoing relevance of Dharma for bringing new perspective, serenity, and healing responses to disequilibrating situations, such as addiction, abortion, adultery, single parenting, and illness.

To begin our journey into the stories, let me share highlights from my own. Born to a Japanese mother and white American father, our home was a space in which the social dynamics and differences of race, language, and culture were intimately baked into everyday life. Our family attended an active social-justice church in downtown Detroit, my mother joining more for family harmony than belief in a transcendent power.

My mother was a survivor. Weeks after she was born, the Great Kanto Earthquake of 1923 occurred. Her father protected her from harm, but his own legs were gravely injured in the process. My mother also managed to survive World War II, learning that you run perpendicular to a bomber flying overhead. Her survival skills were further honed on the streets of metropolitan Detroit, where she was often treated with disdain due to her pronounced Japanese accent and called, among other choice epithets, a yellow belly.

To this day I can still see the dignity that appeared on my mother's dark-skinned face as she held my seven-year-old hand while we walked to an opening in a pew near the pulpit of our unusually crowded Gothic sanctuary on that early spring afternoon of 1968. Dr. Martin Luther King Jr. had come to preach in the aftermath of the 1967 summer riots that ravaged the little part of the world we lived in. I can still feel his voice reverberate in my heart, seared there after I learned he was shot and killed a few weeks later. A neighbor from across the street had been shot and killed, too. Police, fire, and ambulance sirens racing up and down the streets nearby kept me awake knowing that our neighbor and Dr. King were not the only ones in harm's way.

Education was my chosen path to pursue peace and love. While I was a religion major in college, a professor observed that my way of understanding the world was Buddhist. He figured I had learned about it from my mom, but my mom had no conscious awareness that she was imparting Buddhist ways of being. She was mostly concerned that I was polite and kind. I sometimes laugh to myself that I needed a PhD, from Harvard no less, to understand my family.

Meeting a Japanese Zen nun at the site of the Buddha's enlightenment ignited the trajectory of my life, beginning with a thesis-turned-book, *Women Living Zen*.[7] I spent years doing field research in Japan and getting to know the Japanese parts of myself and my family. After giving birth, I shifted my field research focus from nuns to laywomen and the healing rituals that animate and fortify their lives. The fruits of this effort not only involved publishing two more books:[8] The relationships formed in the course of this research were immensely helpful in raising my son and navigating the challenges and vicissitudes of a scholarly life devoted to understanding the hearts of Buddhist women. My daily life now is largely vitalized by Soto Zen practices and teachings, though I freely integrate the wisdom of other approaches. Teaching in a range of educational environments enriches me with experiences and insights that keep me grounded and inspired. My hope is that sharing this constellation of experiences among the myriads of influences that shape me will orient you to what informs my perspective, interpretation, analysis, and imagination.

The stories that follow present women liberating Dharma from patriarchal and misogynist views as well as Dharma liberating women from suffering.

PART ONE

Dharma Women Blossoming in the Past

CREATIVE HISTORIES

A treasure trove of women's motivations, accomplishments, and wisdom in following the Buddhist path is preserved in an ancient anthology of poetry by the earliest Buddhist nuns. Recorded in the Pali language, it is called the *Therigatha*. The *Therigatha* makes plain that from the beginning women in the Buddhist tradition have wielded liberating power. It stretches back orally to the time of the Buddha. It is a rare treasure in terms of historical documents that preserve the earliest Buddhist women's enlightenment experiences. Through their songs we learn how women faced the death of loved ones, making palpable the agony of pain and loss. It gives us access to insights women gleaned from observing their aging bodies. Their hymns of awakening reveal their integrity and awareness as they confess awareness that their own thoughts and actions generate suffering. As a window into how women applied liberative wisdom, the fact of the *Therigatha*'s existence tempers efforts by the patriarchy to suggest women are inferior or less capable of living Dharma and experiencing its liberative fruits.

The *Therigatha* is a constant source of inspiration and affirmation to which I have turned for guidance in writing my stories. It fueled my imagination about how women over two thousand years ago responded with clarity, insight, and spunk. The anthology even includes a story about a nun's stunning response to an unpleasant sexual advance. The nun demonstrates keen wisdom to act in a way that effectively helped a man dissolve the poison of desire and prevent the perpetrator from generating more suffering. The story is a powerful illustration of liberating compassion.

Whether the account is literal or metaphorical, it tells us that among the earliest Buddhist literature, the tradition was aware that women had the courage and perspicacity to respond to unwelcome events by creatively applying Buddhist principles. To view history through a lens wide enough to see women's contributions and their ways of being Buddhist, the historical materials to which we have access are like pieces of a puzzle. Some pieces promise to yield insights into what women did and circumstances they faced. Other pieces give rise to more curiosity about what the missing pieces might look like. We can use the evidence we have to seek these missing pieces out.

Unlike a completed jigsaw puzzle that leaves nothing to the imagination, however, history will always have missing pieces. So, as is done in all presentations of history, I engage the imagination to create plausible stories. I begin each story with introductory information to orient the reader to the sociohistorical context of the story as well as explain what that context illuminates about Buddhist women. I specify which figures and features of the story are historical and which are imaginative. Weaving together these elements as I craft stories highlights women's contributions to history and underscores lacunae in our knowledge of history. It also demonstrates how creating narratives enables one to envision Buddhist teachings, practices, and institutions free from patriarchal and misogynist ways.

1

LETTERS OF LOVING GRATITUDE

Mahaprajapati and Shakyamuni

(FIFTH CENTURY B.C.E., VAISHALI, INDIA)

Becoming a mother myself, it became clear to me that women who have given birth do not need modern feminist theory to tell them that their bodies are powerful sources of life. Our sons and daughters alike traversed our birth canals. Keenly aware of their bodily needs, we nourished our sons and daughters with our breast milk. We encouraged their walking and talking. That some sons grew up and wrote down ideas and prescribed rules that did not respect us does not erase our knowledge that our sons were as dependent on us for their survival as were our daughters. There are no guarantees what a child will do with the care they receive.

Consider how Siddhartha's father so wanted his son to become a wheel turner in the political world that he went to great lengths to shield him from suffering, hoping this would increase the odds his son would not go on a quest to stop suffering. In contrast, women of the era were intimate with suffering: dying in childbirth, nurturing and burying their babies, caring for the sick, and tending to the needs of aged and dying elders. To think that across the twenty-five hundred years of the Buddhist tradition there haven't been women who sought and gained wisdom regarding healing responses to suffering is a hard case to make.

Reliable historical knowledge exists about Mahaprajapati, the woman who led the establishment of the renunciant path for Buddhist women and the first Buddhist woman recognized as enlightened. After the loss of her sister, Maya, the birthmother of Siddhartha, Mahaprajapati followed the social expectation of becoming her sister's husband's wife and the mother of her sister's child. With a king and kingdom watching, there is no evidence that she resisted her situation. Though surely a host of competing emotions coursed through her, it is reasonable to imagine that she integrated these life-altering experiences into her understanding of the nature of the human condition. We can assume that her engagement with life reflected a wise acceptance of the vicissitudes and impermanence of things. It is easy to imagine that she developed an intimate bond with her son, Siddhartha. As he grew up, it is also easy to imagine the tenor of their relationship developed into deep understanding and wholesome respect. Mahaprajapati fully inhabited her life of leadership and attained supreme awakening.

Although it is difficult to determine which details of Siddhartha's life are historical and which are imaginative hagiography, it is widely accepted that he became known as Gautama Buddha. To evoke emotional warmth in the mother-child relationship of these eminent and pivotal historical figures, I crafted letters they might have exchanged. Before Mahprajapati crossed the threshold into "the great, mysterious, unconditioned beyond,"[1] I imagined a letter she might have written to her son, the Buddha:

Dear Son,

Seeing you again fills me with joy. Though it seems only yesterday that I cradled you in my arms heavy with the grief of my sister's, your mother's, tragic and abrupt passing. I think she, too, is beaming with delight that you have indeed become a wheel turner and turned the wheel that promises to liberate all beings from suffering. While you were growing up under the weight of becoming a great king, I was more concerned that you grew to be a person who cared for the well-being of others. When you left the palace, yes, my heart ached to see you go, but I respected your choice and prayed to the gods and goddesses that you would find deep meaning in your quest. I also knew that if you were successful in your quest, you would share it with as many as you could, because you were always serious, open-minded, and thoughtful, even as a young boy. Upon hearing that what you found would help people stop generating suffering, I had to come and learn for myself. Many women decided to join me, and I am grateful that you have accepted us all. I know it takes courage to go against social expectations and even more courage to go against your own father's intent wishes.

The glow of tranquility that emanates from you is proof that what you found and now teach is effective. Your primary insights will surely help many people heal, including me. Though it is plain to see there is suffering in our world, like a doctor, you help us understand the cause and cure for this diagnosis. In pinpointing ignorance about the dynamics of impermanence as the cause of suffering, you give us hope that there is a way out of suffering. There are so many things that we do not have control over in life, but you offer a cure: set our intention to realize enlightenment, deepen our understanding of the nature of reality, and focus our concentration with sustained effort. With our whole body-minds we can speak and act with compassion as we choose livelihoods that are nonharmful to others and entrust our lives to Dharma. No matter how tenuous we might feel, these are things anyone can do.

Even though you are the boy I raised, I am impressed by your wisdom to see a path out of suffering and that you have identified which types of activities will help. The women who came with me from all walks of life already feel their suffering lightening, because no one can stop us from integrating these practices into our lives. Going through life is rife with challenges, but your teachings help us see that oppressive forces do not have the power to prevent us from being compassionate. Your teachings help us see that those who try to limit women, or anyone, do not realize that their ignorance is a primary cause of suffering. Many of the women already understand that even if their husbands demand their subservience and become an obstacle to their entering the path of renunciation, they could still maintain their intention to dissolve their ignorance. No one needs anyone's permission to do so. Our faith will support us.

I am grateful for the prior lifetimes when you were my mother and I was your child, but I am especially grateful for having the karma to see you grow to the heights of human potential. All the hardships involved in you reaching the summit of enlightenment were worth it, for now countless people will be able to awaken from the ignorance that would otherwise bind them to suffering.

Thank you.

Dear Mother,

Thank you for your heartfelt letter. I am profoundly grateful for all that you have done to support me, from holding me in love as an infant to respecting my decision to leave home. That you have joined me on the path of Dharma is more meaningful than words can express. I want to convey gratitude for the things you, my birth mother Maya, and my wife Yashodara have taught me.

Though I was too young when my birth mother died to now remember her face, I feel the lingering traces of her care for me in her womb and her caresses to my infant cheeks. Learning to live with the fact of my birth mother's death propelled me into deep reflection about the nature of life and death. Facing such intimate impermanence helped me understand how birth and death are fluid, to feel the transformation of form. Losing her, however sad, has given me the blessing of two loving mothers, directly experiencing that we are all interrelated.

From you I learned the vital importance of kindness and how deeply healing compassion is. Your leadership has opened up Dharma for women, and I am confident it will continue to bear fruit for ages to come. You are a warm light of wisdom that shines on all beings.

From Yashodara I learned humility. I also learned how tenderness in daily human interaction is fundamental to being a Bodhisattva. She modeled patient generosity. I am still grateful to her for the lifetime in which she gave me five of her seven blue lotuses so that I could make a proper offering to Dipankara Buddha. It is perhaps no coincidence that Dipankara Buddha predicted my future enlightenment because in exchange for the lotuses I agreed to marry her again and again in future lifetimes.[2] *He foresaw how she would help me.*

Indeed, you, my birth mother, and my wife—and the host of women who came to Vaisali to enter the path with you on bare, swollen feet—have been crucial in my life. I want to thank you all for demonstrating the liberating power of Dharma by the way you live your lives. Your excellent efforts help spare some the negative karmic consequences that would befall those who saw women as inferior. Please share this with all the women. May each know that I respect and care about their liberation. I am profoundly grateful for how you supported my liberation, too.

Bowing in gratitude,
Your son

When next they met, Mahaprajapati smiled warmly as she gazed into the Buddha's eyes.

2

PHILOSOPHER QUEEN

Shrimala's Teachings on Wombs

(THIRD CENTURY C.E., SHRAVASTI, INDIA)

Claims that female bodies are a compromised and inferior vehicle for liberation leaked into the Buddhist tradition, staining the Dharma. Such assertions are not compatible with basic Dharma teachings of liberation, such as the third noble truth: "It is possible to end suffering." There is no qualifier that delimits this possibility to beings with certain bodily features. The inclusive teachings on "Buddha womb," or *tathagatagarbha*, are in accord with the third noble truth and advance the teaching that all beings are inherently Buddhas. Yet the concept of *tathagatagarbha* is often treated as a mere philosophical theory, a disembodied doctrine.

When I first saw the title *Sutra of Queen Shrimala of the Lion's Roar* and learned that the sutra centered on teachings on Buddha womb, I was excited about what I might learn about a powerful Buddhist laywoman. It struck me that Buddha womb teachings were ripe for examining a woman's perspective on a woman's capacity to be enlightened in a female body.

Indeed, the *Sutra of Queen Shrimala of the Lion's Roar* delivers the teachings through a woman.[1] It begins with a queen whose parents supported her in learning Dharma and aspired for her to reach enlightenment. The queen's explication of the Buddha womb teaching expresses the womb as a metaphor. In due time, the Buddha proclaimed that the queen's Dharma teachings were excellent. Whether these are historical facts or not, somebody back in third-century C.E. India was willing to present the Buddha proclaiming that a woman had an excellent understanding of Dharma.

The impact that the *Sutra of Queen Shrimala* had on Buddhist history lay more in its influence on subsequent sutras, especially the *Lankavatara Sutra* and *The Awakening of Faith in the Mahayana*. After the *Sutra of Queen Shrimala* entered the Chinese Buddhist stream, the womb metaphor morphed into "Buddha-nature," in keeping with a salient tendency for Chinese translators to render female terms into neutral or masculine ones. The concept of Buddha-nature has become a prominent feature of East Asian Buddhist developments, shorn of gender specificity.

I remind myself that my text-based view of the Buddhist tradition is likely different from the view of those who did not have direct access to texts. Since most people in Buddhist history were not literate, they received Dharma through storytelling and ritual activities. I tried to imagine how a sutra dense with philosophical concepts might be expressed as a story. It is tantalizing to imagine what people might have thought to say to explain the teachings on Buddha womb to women. I placed the story in third-century India, because this early Mahayana sutra was written during that time, likely in the Andhra region of South India. It seemed natural to have the queen offer the teachings to her attendants. I crafted my story by first making a list of the tersely worded philosophical and technical details in the sutra, and then I checked them off each time I found a way to weave them into the story. Save for one quote from the sutra, the conversation I depict between the queen and her female attendants is a creative expedient for bringing the philosophical teachings to life.

Queen Shrimala was delighted, though not surprised, when the dutiful messenger delivered a letter from her parents. They had always cared for her with rich opportunities for growth, never intimating that a daughter was any less capable than a son. Devout Buddhists, they envisioned her aspiring to heights beyond her position at the pinnacle of royalty. Wanting nothing less than her full awakening, they encouraged her to study the Buddha's teachings. In due time, the Buddha predicted she would become the Buddha of Universal Light. He praised her explanation of Dharma: "Excellent! Excellent! Your wisdom and skillful means are most profound and sublime!"[2]

Queen Shrimala's teachings went on to become an authoritative force for the pivotal teachings on tathagatagarbha.

One day, with heads bowed, five female attendants approached Queen Shrimala: "Beloved Queen, in what way may we best serve you?"

"I have called you to my chambers today, because as young women, you may have been treated in ways that make you question your worth," the queen said. "Our world is filled with ignorance. Such defilements conceal the seed of awakening that lies within each of us. Let me share a teaching that has freed me from doubts and delusions. It is called tathagatagarbha, 'womb of the Buddha.' Though its wisdom is lofty, you can integrate it into daily life. The primary thing to do is live virtuously, which requires paying attention to your thoughts and actions, especially if any are motivated by greed or dislike. Such motivations cloud your ability to see clearly.

"One of the hardest things to see clearly is the nature of self, because things are not entirely what they appear to be. Through our senses we see, hear, smell, taste, touch, and think. These senses provide practical information for navigating life. For example, if someone has fallen, you can assist them because you have eyes to see that they have fallen and then use your arms to lift them.

Daily life is full of such opportunities to behave virtuously, and our senses are central to that aim.

"Yet, our senses can lead us astray for they only reveal part of reality. If we live as if our senses inform us about the whole of reality, then we act in ways that are not fully informed. This invariably leads to results we do not want. We inadvertently generate frustration, dissatisfaction, and sometimes anger. In this way, we produce our own suffering."

"Oh, dear queen, we do not want to live that way," one of the attendants said. "How do we become fully informed?"

"You already have all you need," the queen replied. "When you are honest, live with integrity, and sincerely aim to cause no harm to yourself or others, you can trust what emerges from your wombs. They are powerful sources of wisdom. Listen deeply. Wombs provide the conditions for allaying suffering and activating enlightened activity. By definition they generate compassionate care, providing all the nourishment and protection needed to grow and thrive. Indeed, being pregnant is Bodhisattva work. You are cultivating a Buddha in your body. To nurture an embryo of a Buddha is a momentous responsibility. It is also a major contribution to our world.

"Carrying a being in your womb is excellent practice for how to live all the time. Since caring for an embryo is concrete and has high stakes, it can spur you to intently cultivate compassion. Focus your senses on awareness of the conditions you are generating. All your actions affect the embryo. Do not worry, though. You cannot stain the purity of the embryo. Your womb is pure, but you must be careful not to coat it over with defilements, such as exposing it to toxins and intoxicants, being selfish or callous, and getting overly stressed. Please be sure to eat healthy food and get sufficient hydration and sleep. Spend time in nature where you can hear birds sing and feel fresh breezes on your face. Caring for yourself is to care for the Buddha growing in you. To protect yourself from harm creates an environment that protects others from harm. Many women have found that it is easier to be virtuous while pregnant. Their wombs tell them that each action has a direct and immediate consequence on the embryo. Since they are living for another being, they are keenly motivated to be aware and to care.

"Being conscious that the self is not an independent entity is also easier when pregnant. It can help dissolve the delusion of being a separate self. The corporeal connection through the umbilical cord between you and an embryo is direct. In a concrete way, it demonstrates the nature of how all is ultimately interdependently connected."

"Is this teaching helpful if you don't give birth?" one of the attendants asked.

"My beloved, you do not need to have or use a womb for this teaching to be effective," the queen said. "Wombs as perceived through our senses offer only one perspective of reality. Seen through another lens of reality, the womb is the liberating wisdom of emptiness. Through this lens, all boundaries are impermanent, fluid, and ultimately empty of intrinsic substance. Hence, all beings are wombs of Buddhas. Whether you are pregnant or not—have a physical womb or not—you can visualize yourself as pregnant with a Buddha embryo. All your actions can be done with the intent to care for that embryo. Anyone can live with this awareness and cultivate genuine compassion for self and all beings, turning the world into a womb for Buddhas. You enliven this world by nourishing and protecting all beings with loving care.

"Whether you have your own children or not, please share this teaching. It is most important that all our children develop their wisdom. We have the capacity to stop suffering because all our bodies are vehicles for birthing Buddhas."

3

FOOD OF LIBERATION

Mali's Offerings

(FIFTH CENTURY C.E., ANURADHAPURA, SRI LANKA)

When I first chose to focus my scholarship on women in the Buddhist tradition, there was little to be found on the topic. I knew there were numerous books on the male monastic Buddhist tradition, but it took a serendipitous meeting with a Japanese Zen nun in Bodh Gaya, India, in 1987 to open up the world of Buddhist women for me. It was a stunning and transformative meeting. At the time, I was in my sixth year of graduate studies specializing in Japanese Buddhism, and I had not even known there were any Japanese Buddhist nuns. My odyssey into this world began by entering into monastic women's lives. The institutional structure of the community facilitated a focused research project that involved living in a Zen nunnery and talking with the nuns about their motivations. It became my book *Women Living Zen*, which helps balance our understanding of monastic practice by illuminating a women's monastic world.[1]

My next book, *Bringing Zen Home: The Healing Heart of Japanese Women's Rituals*, focused on laywomen. It took fourteen years to produce because the nature of the research required establishing trusting relationships with numerous women who were not in an organized group. Nothing about their lives was published. I had to start with one conversation, followed by many, many more.

Personal connections over time were required to gain insights into the way Dharma affected their lives. These connections also helped me see a whole realm of Buddhist practice that receives insufficient attention, especially in light of how ubiquitous it is. I call it Domestic Dharma[2] because its practitioners are laypeople. I am not suggesting, however, that all practices by lay Buddhists are Domestic Dharma. Domestic Dharma revolves around practices that contribute to caring for a home and its inhabitants. Such practices radiate out from the home as its inhabitants move in the world.

The lacunae in our attention and understanding of domestic life stirred a story in my mind about a laywoman from an earlier period of the Buddhist tradition. I want to draw attention to laywomen because just like Sujata offered rice gruel to Shakyamuni before he attained enlightenment under the bodhi tree, women have cooked food for monastics every single day since Shakyamuni began teaching Dharma. Over twenty-five hundred years—that's a lot of food, making the paucity of information on their lives untenable. My response to this situation was to write a story. I conjured up a vivid image of a woman who devotes a notable amount of her life energy to cooking and offering food for monastics. What might this practice mean to her?

A laywoman would rightfully see herself as an integral part of the Buddhist community, for the community is formally organized into four assemblies. Two assemblies consist of monastic men and women and the other two consist of laymen and laywomen. The relationship of these assemblies is reciprocal. Laity rely on renunciants for teachings based on insights they gain from study and practice. Renunciants rely on laity for much of their food and other material goods that support their effort to focus on spiritual advancement.

The Theravada tradition frames the food offered to renunciants as virtuous action worthy of merit. Although traditionally women cook and offer the food, women's skills, discipline, and commitment to care are rarely highlighted when referencing the practice of almsgiving. Since the inception of the Buddhist tradition, however, women have organized their day to prepare the menu, gather the ingredients, cook the food, serve it, and clean up the dishes afterward, often while tending to the wide-ranging needs of children and the infirm. I want these women to be visible and acknowledged for the essential work they do on behalf of Buddhist communities. The continuous flourishing of the Buddhist tradition is proof of their existence and contributions, but we do not have records of their names. So, I created the fictive characters of Mali, her family, and the monk and framed them in documented geographical, historical, and culinary details.

In the predawn air in a fifth-century Sri Lankan village outside of Anuradhapura,[3] Mali carries a large clay vessel as she heads out to fetch the first water for the day. Usually her sister-in-law, Dipani, did this, but last night she started feeling feverish. Fevers sometimes come and go quickly, and Mali prays that this will be the case for Dipani. At the well, she greets other women from the village and mentions she is there due to her sister-in-law feeling under the weather. Everyone pauses in silence as if to quickly pray the fever be quick, for they each know such things can become bad. They also know what it is like when one set of hands is unavailable to help with the prodigious morning chores.

On Mali's return home, she hears birds begin to sing in the softened light of morning opening. It is actually a treat to be out moving in the morning before the heat of the day, though she does renew her appreciation of how strong Dipani is to carry the water every day. It is so heavy!

After Mali sets down the water, she immediately lights the fire to cook the rice. She makes a mental note to tell her middle son to be sure to bring some firewood in from the pile out back because she would soon need more fuel to cook. Now that he is ten, this is a chore he can handle all by himself. Thanks to the patient guidance her mother-in-law gave when she was first married into the family fourteen years ago, Mali could now matter-of-factly cook the rice for the proper amount needed for each meal. There were twenty-four mouths to feed this morning: seven children and seventeen adults, including eight monks. However, the three younger children and her grandparents-in-law typically ate less than the others. To minimize waste, she calculates the volume accordingly. Given that today her sister-in-law is not feeling well, she considers that, too. As the children grow, she also observes how much more they are eating so she can adjust the quantity of rice. The length of time and amount of water needed to cook the rice varies by volume, and Mali focuses her awareness to make sure the texture is consistent, not too hard, not too soft. She cooks rice three times a day.

Her mother-in-law is renowned for her pickles and chutneys, so she is in charge of preparing them to offer to the monks. Dipani usually makes the curry, but today Mali, her mother-in-law, and Dipani's eldest daughter share the effort. They keep it simple: a basic red lentil dal with spices and coconut milk.[4]

Their family is committed to offering the Venerable monks alms as often as they can.[5] They are blessed to live where they can see the majestic four-hundred-foot-tall Jetavana stupa in the distance.[6] Though it was completed nearly one hundred years ago, their family still talks about making bricks as their contribution to the massive effort to build it. When the project first began, eager children gathered sand a handful at a time, and by the completion of the stupa fifteen years later, they were able to carry as much as any adult. Such stories never grow old because each brick made, carried, and placed was baked with the prayers of the villagers. Brick by brick they helped construct a monumental stupa with their bare hands.

They feel blessed to live practically in the shadow of the largest stupa in the land. Large numbers of monastics live nearby, enriching the palpability of Dharma in daily life.[7] On mornings when Mali feels sluggish from a poor night's sleep, she tells herself, "If the Buddha can awaken to the nature of reality, I can get out of bed!" It never fails to bring immediate joy and infuse her movement with gratitude. Their home is close enough to hear the temple bell announce the time for offering breakfast to the Buddha.[8] This signals to the women in the village that a saffron-robed monk would soon approach to gather alms for himself and other monastics. The women finish preparations and carry out the aromatic pots burgeoning with freshly cooked food to offer.

Mali was sixteen when her mother first took her to join the women to offer food for the Venerables. The women gathering in their sarees of yellows, greens, and reds reminded her of colorful flowers consecrating an altar for the Buddha. To finally be included in this virtuous ritual that shaped the flow of their lives was an acknowledgment of their faith in her. Although as a child she had helped to prepare food for the Venerables, it was a sign that she was recognized as a woman to offer food directly into the large alms bowl one Venerable would take to share with fellow monks. Her immense respect for the Venerable's dedication to Dharma made her a little nervous as she used the large serving spoon to put rice into his alms bowl. Being so close to someone who meditated, chanted in Pali, and could read the Lord Buddha's words in the suttas was an honor.

The Venerable who came that morning to gather alms kept his eyes downcast as the women put food into the bowl. He looked to be the age of her older brother and made her wonder how this Venerable was able to know the celibate life of a monk was for him. Just as Mali thought that, he raised his gaze and their eyes met for a flash. It sounded like thunder in her heart. Later she realized it was likely because she was new to the offering line, but she wondered if it was hard for him to receive food from a woman's hand.

To this day, each of the fifteen years of mornings since that first day, Mali still finds deep satisfaction in putting the rice she just cooked into the spacious alms bowl as the Venerable files past her. She wondered if Sujata felt the same contentment, not knowing if the person she was feeding rice porridge to was going to be a Buddha. Supporting such earnest people makes Mali's days more meaningful. It makes her a stronger, more caring and thoughtful person to wake up extra early to cook and offer them rice. Though she does not have interest in meditating, Mali knows in her heart that her rice is an essential contribution to the community of awakening.

After they offer the food to the Venerable, the family gathers to eat their breakfast. Mali, however, first gets a bowl of rice left over from the night before. She deliberately saves some every day just in case someone wakes up not feeling well. She pours in some freshly pressed coconut milk, as her mother taught her that the cold soup of rice and milk was good for someone who was not feeling well.

Despite Dipani's earlier gesture of trying to help when the hecticness of getting the food ready in time for the monks' alms crescendoed, she eventually surrendered and went back to resting in bed. With a smile, Mali gently helps Dipani sit up and hands her the bowl of soup. They exchange a knowing look. They both understand that resting is the fastest way for Dipani to return to her feet and that Dipani would do the same for Mali when she was not feeling well. It seemed forever ago when Mali first joined this family. Dipani had become a true sister.

The older kids help clean up the kitchen after breakfast and oversee the younger children's morning chores. Her daughter, Sumana, is becoming increasingly helpful. She knows how to gather the banana leaves they need to serve food. Mali had always loved that chore when she was a young girl, so seeing Sumana blossom in this role brought a smile to her face. Her mother-in-law goes out to the garden to do some weeding and see what vegetables are ready for eating for dinner. Mali grabs a young coconut so she can give

Dipani something refreshing to drink. Her mother-in-law comes back in with a basket of yams and beans. They decide to boil yams, which with freshly grated coconut makes for a simple but filling dish. Mali asks her eldest daughter to grate some fresh coconuts, so they will be ready to prepare lunch. They also decide dinner would be a curry of cashews, yams, and beans cooked in coconut milk with the basic mix of spices: turmeric, cumin, curry leaves, cinnamon, and cardamom.

As the sun starts sinking into the horizon, setting the stupa aglow in golden light, Mali goes to check on Dipani. She is relieved to find Dipani's fever has broken. The children are running around riling up the chickens, the squawking and laughter blending into a cacophony of cheer. Mali starts thinking about what they should next cook for the Venerables, warmed by the thought that the children are being raised in a world where people help each other.

4

LEADING AND BOWING

Dharma Offerings of Empress Wu and Nun Lianlu

(SEVENTH CENTURY C.E., CHANG-AN, CHINA)

Empress Wu (624–705), the founder of the Zhou dynasty, contributed significantly to the development of the Buddhist tradition in China in the seventh century, and her life demonstrates the ways a woman historically wielded Dharma. For the following story, I imagined a nun, Lianlu, a contemporary of Empress Wu, who reflects on the momentous sociohistorical events of her time in light of Buddhist teachings and practices. She intimates creative ways contemporary women might also liberate Dharma from patriarchal practices and misogynist teachings. By intricately weaving together historical and imagined people, events, and texts, I aim to expand our view of the history of Buddhist women and the possibilities of invoking their wisdom to address inequities today.

Exploring a woman's perspective of Buddhist doctrines that demean women casts a stark light on the irrationality upon which they depend. Buddhist sutras often embed direct contradictions, as does the *Sutra on Transforming the Female Body*, the medieval Chinese sutra that promulgated the notion that all beings are empty of intrinsic substance yet has the Buddha purport that women would benefit from transforming their bodies into male bodies.[1] Empress Wu, who was a Buddhist nun before embarking on a path that would result in her leading the country and establishing Buddhism as the state religion, proved that she could see through the unsubstantiated assertions of such unreasonable teachings. She would have encountered such teachings in her training at Ganye Temple, a prominent temple in the Tang dynasty capital of Chang-an.[2] She demonstrated her philosophical and political acumen by seriously engaging with subtle and abstract philosophical teachings and wielding them to cut through patriarchal institutions to rise to the summit of political power. She defied pronouncements found in sutras that assert a woman could not be a chakravartin, a leader of political or spiritual realms. A devoted and consequential supporter of Buddhist practices and teachings, Empress Wu and astute Buddhist teachers around her discerned that she was the woman scriptures announced would rule the country as a chakravartin, assisting her ascent to the pinnacle of spiritual and political power and reign over the Zhou dynasty.

The historical personages in my story include Empress Wu, her two husbands—Emperor Taizong (598–649 C.E.) and his son, Emperor Gaozong (628–683 C.E.)—her nephew, and the renowned Buddhist teacher Fazang (643–712 C.E.). All locations are actual. All the sutras exist except for sutras my fictive nun, Lianlu, envisaged and revised. All historical events occurred except for events that unfold from the imagined meeting of Empress Wu and Lianlu, including them hearing teachings together and Lianlu's pilgrimage with her disciples to pay homage to Empress Wu. All Buddhist teachings and practices are authentic except for those in Lianlu's imagined sutra writings.

My story unfolds from the viewpoint of Lianlu. Through my fictive nun's eyes, we can reflect on the experience, perspective, and ideas of a seventh-century nun in Chang-an because the sociohistorical context in which I place the story is based on documented information.

The Silk Road funneled products, people, and practices from the far west and sundry regions of Eurasia through Chang-an, the capital of the Tang dynasty (618–690 and 705–907 C.E.). In the seventh century, Chang-an was a buzzing cosmopolitan city that was central to driving a period of rich growth. Not coincidentally, women of Chang-an enjoyed freedom. They were known to be confident and competent in numerous activities that fueled the culture. It was in this context that a woman wielded her prodigious skills to actualize her vision of becoming ruler of the country.

Wu Zhao (624–705 C.E.)[3]—the woman who would become China's first recorded ruling empress—became a widow at age twenty-five when Emperor Taizong died in 649. As his royal consort with no children, she followed the tradition of entering the esteemed Ganye Temple to become a Buddhist nun.[4]

At the same time, another woman, aged twenty-four, entered the temple. She, too, was widowed young. It was not unusual for a widow from an aristocratic family to choose to become a nun or for the family she had married into to raise her infant son. She was given the Dharma name Lianlu (Lotus Dew).

A nun's life was a quiet one with a measured pace. The two young, widowed novices learned its daily rhythms together, both particularly enjoying chanting sutras with the fragrance of incense wafting through the air. Due to the high stature of Ganye Temple, they learned about Dharma from erudite and wise teachers. The two nuns found the teachings on the relationship of form and emptiness an especially intriguing challenge. One of the teacher's simple explanations was most helpful. As snow was gently falling, the elder nun asked her protégés to look out to the garden, where a plum blossom was blooming. She pointed out how rain had fallen earlier and nourished the tree to grow. Now that the temperatures were colder, though, snow rather than rain fell. Since there is no fixed essence to water, its form is dependent on particular conditions.

The teacher gave other common examples of things that are dependent on specific conditions to arise: leaves changing color in the cool autumn nights, the moon waxing and waning as it orbits the earth, or the vegetables that only grow in the summer. They came to see the causes and conditions of phenomenal reality and how everything is interrelated in an ever-transforming stream of impermanence.

The elder nun also asked a series of questions that focused on their own bodies. What have they eaten to nourish their bodies? Where did the food come from? Where is that food now? After the teacher noted that we can see differences of form in male and female bodies, she pressed her students to consider if a peach becomes female when a woman eats it. Does a peach become male when a man eats it? Is skin male or female? Are bones male or female? She ended the lesson with a teaching from the *Sutra on Transforming the Female Body*: "In all dharmas there is neither male nor female!"[5]

A few years into their life as Buddhist nuns, their temple held a service in memory of Emperor Taizong. Emperor Gaozong attended it in honor of his father. This occasioned Wu Zhao to renew communications with him. Although it was not typical for a royal consort to ordain and then return to palace life, Wu Zhao did. She eventually had four sons and was elevated to the highest rank of consort. As the Heavenly Empress ruling alongside Emperor Gaozong, she continued to be devoted to Buddhism and became a generous patron that supported its growth in numerous ways. Her 675 patronage that contributed to the massive Buddhist stone carvings in Luoyang's Longmen Grottoes[6] was a harbinger of her future. After Emperor Gaozong passed in 683, Wu Zhao eventually founded the Zhou dynasty with Luoyang as its capital and reigned as Holy and Divine Empress from 690 to 705.

Empress Wu focused on uplifting women's rights and advanced the idea that an ideal ruler is one who rules as a mother rules over her children.[7] To deepen her understanding of Buddhist teachings, she asked Huayan Buddhist master Fazang to explain the *Huayan Sutra* to her.[8] To convey the primary teaching of interpenetration—"all in one and one in all"—he lit a candle in an octagonal hall he built of eight mirrors, adding a mirror on the top and bottom. The light of the one candle shone clearly in each mirror, which demonstrated that everything is present in each part, an interrelated and interdependent whole. Such teachings helped her see the hollowness of men claiming superiority over women, fortifying her aim to reign over the country as a mother.

Despite there being no record of a woman reigning over China before, a Buddhist text that circulated in 690—*The Commentary on the Meanings of the Prophecies About the Divine Sovereign in the Great Cloud Sutra*—supported Empress Wu's sovereignty.[9] The commentary imparts that the *chakravartin* (universal wheel-turning monarch) in the *Great Cloud Sutra* referred to Empress Wu.[10] In the *Great Cloud Sutra*, the Buddha proclaims that Devi of Pure Radiance, who appeared as an earthly queen, would "reign over the territory of a country in the body of a woman."[11] Indeed, on October 5, 693, led by Empress Wu's nephew, thousands of people requested that she add the embellished august title "Cakravartin of the Golden Wheel" to her already grand designation, "Sagely and Divine Emperor."[12] Empress Wu promulgated *The Commentary* throughout the empire to herald the scriptural basis and verification of her spiritual authority.[13]

Empress Wu expressly enjoined monastics to transmit its teachings, which is how those at Ganye Temple heard this text. Learning of the wondrous eminence of the new ruler of the country prompted Lianlu to reflect on the time she spent with Empress Wu when they were novice nuns forty-five years earlier. She decided to gather a group of her disciples and go on a pilgrimage to pay homage to their chakravartin empress in her capital of Luoyang. She also wanted to see with her own eyes and share with her disciples the sight of the giant Vairocana Buddha carved into the Longmen Grottoes that the empress helped develop.[14]

They waited until 697 to begin their pilgrimage because they received news that the majestic, 285-foot-tall Mingtang (Bright

Hall) had burned in a fire.[15] They awaited the completion of the reconstruction and timed their departure for a moderate season. Finally, in mid-spring of 697, they set off. Lianlu had recently turned seventy-two. Her disciples were determined to care for their beloved teacher on this momentous 230-mile journey. The distance was not all on flat land, and they planned to rest for a few days at temples along the way. Weather and health permitting, they anticipated it would take six to eight weeks to reach Luoyang from Chang-an.

The long days of walking afforded Lianlu time to consider matters in a deep and extended fashion. Along the way, when the nuns encountered a monk, they bowed to him, for the nuns adhered to the eight extra *Garudharma* rules for nuns, one of which stated, "A nun who has been ordained even for a hundred years must greet respectfully, rise up from her seat, salute with joined palms, do proper homage to a monk ordained but that day."[16]

Although Lianlu harbored doubts about nuns bowing to monks in a unilateral practice, she yielded to it since she found that bowing helped her dissolve the tenacious delusion of being a separate self. She found bowing itself, no matter the context, embodied humility. Bowing reminded her that she is an integral part of a vast web of activity pulsing with both suffering and compassion. Bowing generated an experience of trust in the interconnected whole. For her, each bow refreshed her awareness of all for which she was grateful.

One day when they encountered a young monk walking alone toward them, Lianlu paused and looked directly into the monk's face. Though it was highly unusual for a nun to look squarely at an unknown monk's face, Lianlu recognized the features of this young monk. He looked like her deceased husband. Though she had not seen her son since she left for the temple when she was twenty-four, she had heard that he eventually married and had a son of his own. This young monk looked like he could be her grandson. Since they were both renunciants, she did not inquire.

The encounter prompted Lianlu to ponder how the practice of nuns unilaterally bowing to monks might affect monks, especially young ones. As they continued on their journey, she had time to consider that, in a world ruled by the first female emperor, maybe it wasn't right for a woman to bow to a man just because he was a man. Not only did the practice contradict the cosmopolitan ethos of women engaging in numerous activities that had been the province of men, but it also struck her that the practice might be detrimental to monks. The concern grew heavy in her heart as she contemplated what those like her grandson would learn from the practice. If elder nuns continuously bowed down to him for no other reason than they are female and he is male, might it be harder for him to maintain awareness that he is not only not special but that women are equally capable of liberating wisdom? Lianlu worried that these young monks' efforts to live in accord with the Dharma teaching of no-self were being undermined by nuns treating them in a way that exalted them and perhaps cultivating a delusion in them that men were superior to women, resulting in them treating nuns as if they were not able to fathom Dharma as well as a monk.[17]

Fortified by the positive view of women she had recently heard from *The Commentary* Emperor Wu promulgated, Lianlu thought back to the passage from the *Sutra on Transforming the Female Body* that she had learned with Empress Wu all those years ago. "In all dharmas there is neither male nor female!" And yet, that same sutra also urged women to change into men. It had always confused Lianlu how a teaching based fundamentally on emptiness could advocate for such a thing, and she had never been persuaded by the ten reasons the sutra offered for why women would be better off as men. Given the rhetoric of this sutra and her concern for monks being unilaterally bowed to, Lianlu thought of a way to counterbalance any reifying tendencies that might encourage delusions about the nature of bodies that arise from such texts and practices.

While walking along in silence, she mentally composed a *Sutra on Transforming the Male Body*. She decided the *Sutra on Transforming the Male Body* would mirror the *Sutra on Transforming the Female Body* with a similar but opposite admonition: "I command my man's body to transform into a female one!"[18] Likewise, as the *Sutra on Transforming the Female Body* volunteers ten reasons why women need to change into men, she conjured up ten reasons why a male best transform into a female:[19]

1. Men cannot be pregnant and therefore cannot nurture and care for another being growing in their own body, missing the advantage of understanding the illusory nature of independent existence that sharing one's body with another human being provides.
2. Men cannot give birth and therefore cannot experience how the pain of childbirth can awaken the Bodhisattva virtues of patience, generosity, and diligence.
3. Men lack functional breasts, so they cannot nurse a baby with their own body and don't experience the joy and confidence that attends having such a bodily power.
4. Such inabilities give rise to insecurity and weakness,
5. Which in turn results in men trying to hide them through being boastful and arrogant.
6. Being closed to others' views and unwilling to listen to others gives rise to spiritual complacency.
7. Men are competitive and combative rather than cooperative.
8. Men are divisive rather than harmonious.
9. Men are lustful.
10. Men are shortsighted rather than thinking of future generations.

Lianlu thought an amendment to the *Golden Light Sutra* would be helpful, too. With this sutra she substituted "women" for "men":

> May all men be transformed into women,
> Courageous, intelligent, and full of wisdom.
> May they practice the Bodhisattva path at all times,
> Cultivating the Six Perfections until they reach the realm of enlightenment.[20]

Lianlu envisioned that if men and women studied both versions of these sutras, they might be spared delusions about the nature of bodies and self. She was not ready to declare that these sutras were not in accord with the Dharma teachings on emptiness, but she did decide to teach her new ideas to her disciples once they completed their pilgrimage.

After weeks of walking, Lianlu and her disciples reached Luoyang as a dim glow from the setting sun hovered over the capital. They rested a night so they would be fresh and strong to pay proper respect to Empress Wu. At sunrise, they walked toward the palace. They could see the Bright Hall rising into the heavens through tears that welled up at the immensity of what they saw. They deeply breathed in the significance of what it meant. With all the gravity, respect, and gratitude they could imbue into their nine prostrations—full body stretched out onto the earth—they bowed to Empress Wu as their political and spiritual female chakravartin.[21]

Exalted to affirm they were alive in an era of female liberation, the nuns continued to the Longmen Grotto where thousands of Buddhist figures were carved in the steep limestone cliffs along the Yi River. In seeing Vairocana Buddha towering fifty-six feet above her, awe rippled through Lianlu's body. Facing the serene countenance of the Cosmic Buddha, she moved closer, feeling its warmth and powerful protection. She noted an uncanny resemblance to her fellow novitiate, now Empress Wu. Lianlu smiled when later she heard other pilgrims murmur that the Empress's face served as an inspiration for this glorious Buddha that featured exquisite refinements.[22] With ears nearly seven feet long, Lianlu mused that Vairocana must hear all the sounds of Dharma throughout the universe.

Vairocana's presence was palpable as the small group of nuns offered various chants and did nine full prostrations toward his lotus throne. Sitting in the shadow of Vairocana Buddha with her disciples, Lianlu shared the reverie she had along the pilgrimage route regarding the practice of nuns bowing unilaterally to monks and her idea to minimize suffering by revising and composing a sutra. Her disciples' insight into the nature of emptiness and its relation to form deepened, kindling their inspiration to share this with men and women far and wide. Riding on the winds of change in the air with a reigning empress, they imagined that special preference for a specific gender would melt away into a narrower period of history, and their current insights would be passed down through the generations. The male bias and discrimination against women found in some sutras and practices would be remedied, protecting others from having to suffer as they did.

5

COMPASSION PERSONIFIED

Empress Kōmyō and Women of Hokkeji Temple

(THIRTEENTH CENTURY C.E., NARA, JAPAN)

Thirteenth-century Japan saw a resurgence of female monastic activity that emanated from a historically important nuns' temple in Nara known for attracting numerous laywomen and female pilgrims to its gates: Hokkeji (Lotus Temple).[1] Centering my story on this temple illuminates the qualities and activities that a Japanese nuns' temple cultivates and how women's lives in thirteenth-century Nara, Japan, were affected by a nun's temple in their midst. Grounding the story with historical figures and locations for which we have documentation aids in discerning plausible ways people might have thought, felt, and interacted. The historical figures featured in this story are Empress Kōmyō (701–760 C.E.), Hokkeji abbess Jizen (b. 1187 C.E.), and Chōgen (1121–1206 C.E.), a high-ranking monk who funded a major restoration of Hokkeji buildings.

Augmenting the historical context with imagined characters facilitates appreciation of the lived immediacy and inner lives of those for whom we have little to no documentation. In this story, I created a farming family (Kiku, her sister, and her son, Taka); a woman from an artisanal family, Chikako; two nuns at Hokkeji (Jikō and Sanshin); three people from an aristocratic background (Lady Tsubaki, her deceased husband, and her son); and Lady Tsubaki's attendant. Kiku's farm is in an actual farming locale, and Lady Tsubaki's estate is in an area of Kyoto where aristocrats lived, near Tōfukuji Temple in the southeast part of Kyoto. All other locations, temples, and shrines actually exist. The practices, Buddhist rites, types of activities, and events of my tale are based on historically documented practices and observances, though I have my imagined people enact them with sensibilities conceivable for thirteenth-century Japan. Intertwining these historical and fictive people enables me to create intimate interactions between different spheres of people and to explore several dimensions of thirteenth-century Japanese Buddhist women's lives. Outside the temple, these figures would not have much opportunity to cross paths. Yet inside the temple, they find a common haven.

Nara was the capital of Japan (710–794 C.E.) when Empress Kōmyō founded Hokkeji in 741. Motivated by her vision to spread compassion and protection throughout the land, Empress Kōmyō provided the temple with significant support during her lifetime. After she passed, though, political tides shifted, resulting in the end of state support.[2] The temples led by monks, however, continued to receive funding.

Despite this uneven treatment, the nuns continued Empress Kōmyō's legacy of compassion and maintained the temple as a locale for people to find healing in their times of need. Having that original imperial support facilitated Hokkeji's inclusion in a Nara-based pilgrimage. The melding of Kannon (Bodhisattva of Compassion) and Empress Kōmyō's compassion drew people to the temple gates. That the nuns kept the temple running through the centuries is testimony to their dedication, discipline, and sincerity. Although the physical structures of the temple have changed, today, nearly eight centuries later, the temple still stands with dignity on the plains surrounded by undulating green mountains.

The warm and caring quality of the nuns' temple and their responsiveness to women's concerns are reflected in the following story I wove. Imagine with me how nuns opened their temple doors and their hearts to support those who sought refuge, healing, and peace. I created these characters to walk you into this world.

Kiku was born in 1198. She grew up on a farm down the road from Hokkeji, an imperial nunnery founded during the Nara period by Empress Kōmyō. Empress Kōmyō designated it the head *kokubunniji*—the highest-ranking official state nunnery in Japan.[3] The temple was a ten-minute walk to the east of Nara's Imperial Palace. Modeled after Chang-an—the capital of the Tang dynasty in China—the area exuded a sense of serene organization and nobility.

Hokkeji was designated the sister temple to Tōdaiji, the monumental temple built about two miles to the east. Renowned for its giant bronze Vairocana Buddha, the temple was a calm yet powerful presence in the ancient capital. Tōdaiji was appointed the head temple of all provincial temples. When the capital moved to Kyoto, however, nuns continued to live and practice at Hokkeji, though state support ended. The palace grounds were left to decay, and the land was used for agriculture. Several generations before Kiku was born, her family farmed the land that had once been the grounds of the Imperial Palace.

In rhythm with the monastic life, the farmers in the area rose to the tolling of Hokkeji's temple bell just before dawn and began to rest when they heard its deep sonority undulate through the sky at sunset. During the day they tended to their fields of yams and barley. When the breeze was just right, they could faintly smell the temple's incense wafting by. They were grateful to live near the nuns, for their presence filled the community with virtuous discipline and caring warmth.

Kiku had always been impressed with the resilient, creative, and dedicated nuns who lived and practiced at Hokkeji. She remembers growing up listening to her mother and neighbors tell stories of how the nuns had persevered for nearly four hundred years without financial support from the state, even though their brother temple received funding. The story never got old. From the vantage point of the farmers in the area, the nuns proved their genuine motivation to be Buddhist monastics and live Dharma, for they did not gain material benefits for their effort. The buildings, though, had become a bit run-down. Kiku's mother mentioned that an apparently high-ranking monk named Chōgen, who was dedicated to repairing damage at Tōdaiji, had generously decided to help repair Hokkeji's stupa, main hall, the main Buddhist statue on the altar, and the statues of two attendants.[4] Kiku was only five then, too young to remember those days, so she only really knew Hokkeji in its restored condition.

Not long before Hokkeji's restoration, everyone was thrilled that a Nara pilgrimage developed. Most in the area, however, had been to the sites before they were designated as part of the pilgrimage route that began with Kasuga Shrine and the august Kōfukuji Temple. The third location on the circuit was Tōdaiji, and the people were proud that the Nara pilgrimage route was extended to include Hokkeji as the fourth site.[5]

Legends of the beloved Empress Kōmyō drew pilgrims to Hokkeji. Miracle stories merged Kōmyō and Kannon in the hearts and minds of devotees, especially as embodied in the exquisite Eleven-Headed Kannon at Hokkeji.[6] Bringing their refined understanding of the power of beauty, aristocratic women often came on pilgrimage to behold the elegant statue. Each of the pilgrims' offerings and prayers infused the temple life with benevolence and gratitude.

Kiku's family regularly offered food to the pilgrims who came to Hokkeji, and they welcomed them to rest under a shade tree at the edge of their farm. Now that Kiku and her younger sister were ten and eight, respectively, they were finally entrusted with going to the temple to offer some freshly picked vegetables. They had learned they must always bow when they arrived at the gate of the temple, whether or not anyone could see them. Bowing was not only an expression of respect; it also prepared their hearts and bodies to move with reverence. When they walked into the temple garden, they happened to overhear a nun called Jikō telling pilgrims a story of Empress Kōmyō.

"After the empress built Hokkeji," Jikō said, "she heard a voice from the heavens instruct her to build a healing bathhouse. Upon its completion she readied the hot water. The empress then vowed to 'personally scrub the dirt off the first person who came to bathe that day.'[7] The vow was fresh off her lips when a person in deplorable condition from an area known for outcasts entered the bathhouse. He requested, 'Please scrub my back.' Noting the empress's hesitation, he said, 'If you do not scrub my dirt away yourself, then you will end up tarnishing your vow.' Calming her heart, she reached out to scrub him. Afterward, the man requested she not tell anyone, and she promised not to. Then he emitted a light that fragranced the space rising into the heavens. It turned out he was Ashuku (Akṣobhya) Buddha. The empress made the bathhouse into a temple to memorialize the event. You can see the ruins of the original bathhouse as well as the newer one."[8]

Although the girls grew up hearing the story, this was their first time hearing it directly from a nun. Being on the temple grounds made the story come to life. It did feel like Empress Kōmyō was still caring for everyone, especially the sick. Indeed, everyone in the area knew that if you got sick, you were to go to Hokkeji for healing blessings.

Ten years later, Kiku's first son, Taka—a ruddy-cheeked six-month-old—got a fever that would not come down even after wiping his body down with a damp cloth and placing another on his forehead. A new mother, Kiku was distraught when after a few days of fighting the fever, he became listless. Though she usually carried him around strapped to her back so her hands were free to work, she couldn't bear not to see his face for any signs of change in his condition. So she strapped him to her chest. Still tying the strap around her waist, she headed out the door to go to Hokkeji.

Holding her precious baby, it felt like the walk to the temple took an eternity. Though everything in her wanted to get to the temple as fast as possible, she dared not run. She did not want to jostle him and cause more discomfort. Arriving at the temple, Jikō, a nun she had come to know well, heard the baby crying and came into the worship hall to find Kiku holding Taka in her arms, tears streaming down her face. Jikō lit some incense and sat with Kiku in front of the altar. The statue of Kannon looked down on them with benevolence. With hands in prayer, she bowed and began chanting things Kiku did not understand but could feel were powerful. Then Kiku voiced her prayer that Empress Kōmyō would heal her son. Kiku vowed to offer food to the temple every full moon.

On the next full moon, with buoyant joy and gratitude, Kiku carried her now chipper son on her back with her arms full of vegetables to offer to Hokkeji.

In 1243 a new abbess arrived at Hokkeji. At fifty-six, Jizen was confident, competent, and knowledgeable.[9] Being from an aristocratic family, she brought a wealth of resources with her. Highly educated and refined, she studied and practiced with diligence. In those days, Hokkeji had thirteen nuns,[10] and it was mostly known for being a site of Kōmyō devotion.[11] Though Kōmyō devotion continued, Abbess Jizen was dedicated to tightening the ritual and study schedule at Hokkeji. The nuns chanted extensively three times a day: morning, midday, and evening. Their level of education was evident in that their chants were in several different languages: Chinese, Sanskrit, hybrid Sino-Japanese, and Japanese.[12] They also studied and chanted a highly philosophical scripture of the Yogacara school of philosophy, which indicated the serious depth of their engagement with Buddhist teachings.[13] Demonstrating the extent of their sincerity to live Dharma, the nuns did seated meditation every evening after chanting, a rare practice at temples. The nuns also cared for pilgrims and the local laity as part of their devotion to Dharma.

One autumn day, a laywoman in her fifties, Chikako, came to Hokkeji. She had occasionally attended major rituals, so the nun who cared for lay guests, Sanshin, knew that Chikako had married into a local family on the outskirts of Nara that made tatami mats. On that day, Chikako was clearly distressed. She kept her head down as Sanshin brought her into a small room for some tea and privacy. Before Sanshin could ask her what matter brought her to the temple, Chikako bowed with her forehead to the tatami floor. Though speaking with polite verbal expressions, her trembling voice and body spoke volumes about a raw and rough encounter she must have experienced. When she raised her head, Sanshin saw the purplish shadows on Chikako's face. Unfortunately, this was not the first time Sanshin faced a woman coming to the temple seeking refuge from a violent relationship.

Abbess Jizen came in to speak with Chikako about her situation. Chikako had endured decades of intermittent outbursts of abuse from her husband, and now that her last child was married and safely out of the house, she decided to leave. Abbess Jizen prompted Sanshin to prepare a place for Chikako to stay at the temple for a few weeks. After Chikako had a chance to think carefully and deeply in a safe environment, they would consider what her best path forward might be.[14]

Despite it being winter, an aristocratic lady-in-waiting, Lady Tsubaki,[15] came on pilgrimage to Hokkeji in 1244. She was grieving. Her seventy-seven-year-old husband had died on the twenty-eighth day of the ninth month of 1243. Lady Tsubaki did all the rituals through the one-hundredth day. On the tenth day of the first month of 1244, she set forth on her pilgrimage. Her family was concerned about her going at her advanced age, but she was determined to walk. A trusted attendant assisted her until she settled in at Hokkeji. They spent a night in Uji, which was about halfway between their estate in Kyoto near the newly built Tōfukuji Temple and her first stop on the pilgrimage route in Nara. They spent a day at each pilgrimage site in the traditional order, starting with Kasuga Shrine and moving on to Kōfukuji Temple, then the grand Tōdaiji Temple. They rested on days in between. Finally, they went to Hokkeji.

As they approached the gate of the temple, Kiku and her son, Taka, happened to be going to the temple to deliver the vegetables she had vowed to offer every month in gratitude for saving her then infant son. Now a twenty-six-year-old man, he often went with her for these monthly visits to Hokkeji. They bowed as they waited for Lady Tsubaki to enter the gates first. The attendant bowed back and offered that Lady Tsubaki had come on pilgrimage from Kyoto, planning to stay at the temple for a month.[16] He, however, would be returning to Kyoto forthwith.

Lady Tsubaki had wanted to go to the temple of Kōmyō devotion because she had had a vision of Kōmyō a year ago. She felt it was Kōmyō beckoning her to come to Hokkeji after her husband passed. It helped Lady Tsubaki prepare her heart for her husband's passing and increased her fervor for following the Buddhist path. Daily chanting saw her through this period. Now she was finally at Hokkeji. She wept as she felt the empress's presence through the Eleven-Headed Kannon enshrined at the temple.

The Hokkeji nuns welcomed Lady Tsubaki. They were accustomed to having women of her station stay on retreat with them. Such guests were free to choose which practices to join. Lady Tsubaki sometimes woke up early to join in the morning chanting service and sometimes the evening's as well. A few times early in her visit she even joined them in zazen after evening service.[17] She always joined the midday service, though.[18] She especially enjoyed the afternoon chants because they included the ones she had done at home that focused on Kannon: the rather long *Kannongyo*,[19] five rounds of the energizing "Thousand-Armed [Kannon] Dharani,"[20] and thirty-three rounds of "Eleven-Headed [Kannon] Great Incantation."

One afternoon, Lady Tsubaki was walking through the temple garden as Kiku came to the temple to offer her freshly picked vegetables. Lady Tsubaki bowed her head to Kiku as they passed each other. Kiku bowed low in response as she silently prayed that some of the vegetables she grew would help nourish this devout woman. Kiku had heard she was recently widowed and a dedicated Buddhist. This elegant woman was one of several aristocratic women she has seen over the years come to the nuns' temple for a retreat.

Kiku also met Chikako, who was in the kitchen and received the vegetables Kiku brought. Chikako's hair was now cut to shoulder length, indicating she had made her decision. She confirmed that she had fully committed her life to the Buddhist path. Having had time to live without fear gave her a chance to gain clarity about her values. She was moving into a new identity and phase of life. Having taken the eight pure precepts and ten major Bodhisattva precepts, she was thrilled to formally be a lay follower.[21] Chikako spoke with enthusiasm about someday becoming tonsured and her aspiration to be a full *bikuni* nun. As a lay follower, she served the temple doing a range of necessary but less-than-pleasant tasks, including caring for the bodily remains of the dead.[22] Kiku reflected on how she met many people from a broad cross section of society through the temple, especially the stream of pilgrims from afar. She felt grateful that she lived near this vibrant nuns' temple, for as a farmer she would not normally have had such rich social encounters.

As Lady Tsubaki's month at Hokkeji was drawing to a close, she keenly felt how chanting with others generated a profoundly moving and subtle connection between the nuns, herself, and the Dharma. Breathing together synchronized their heartbeats.

Attuning to each other vitalized them in powerful waves of healing currents. Lady Tsubaki felt her grief flow through and a peace emerge. Although she was still sad about the loss of her husband, and she sensed she was not long for this world, Lady Tsubaki felt a quiet acceptance of these realities. She felt no resistance. Rather, she felt the most exquisite gratitude. When she first decided to come spend a month at Hokkeji, she had no idea this was why.

After the midday chanting service that day, she felt she needed some rest. She did not want to burden the nuns, so she remained quiet about the weakness that was seeping into her bones. She told the nuns she would retire to her room to rest. She moved with such grace that the nuns attributed her measured movement and gentleness to her aristocratic background and her elder age. When the nuns checked in on Lady Tsubaki, she managed to drink some tea. When they came again, they noted how her breathing had grown somewhat feeble. The nuns prayed to Kannon for her.

When in the morning Lady Tsubaki appeared notably fragile, they realized that she was likely near her time. Sanshin ran to Kiku's home, knowing that her son, Taka, was now a strong young man. Sanshin asked if Taka would run to Kyoto to dispatch Lady Tsubaki's son to come to Hokkeji. With urgency pounding in his heart, Taka arrived at Lady Tsubaki's estate by midafternoon. Grateful for Taka's effort to come so swiftly on foot, they offered him rest for the night while Lady Tsubaki's son mounted his horse and sped to Hokkeji.

Evening light was succumbing to the night as the sound of a galloping horse grew closer. Kiku was at the temple. She had brought some vegetables with her, wanting to know how Lady Tsubaki was doing. Kiku was relieved Lady Tsubaki's son arrived in time, having felt partially responsible since it was her son that was sent to deliver the message. Sanshin went out to greet him and usher him to the room where his mother was lying. A hushed cadence of "Namu Shakamuni Butsu" drifted through the air.[23]

Sanshin had placed a scroll painting of *Fugen Raigo* on the wall where Lady Tsubaki could see it. Most nuns of Hokkeji, including Abbess Jizen, were from aristocratic cultures where women preferred aspiring to rebirth in Tushita Heaven.[24]

Lady Tsubaki's breath became calm when she saw her son. An expression of tranquility appeared on her face as she gazed upon the painting of Fugen descending from Tushita Heaven mounted on a white elephant. She felt his protective strength. Accompanied by his retinue floating down on a cloud, she felt her body become light as if she, too, were carried along with them, her long hair trailing.

Closing her eyes, a tear rolled down Lady Tsubaki's cheek. Reaching out to touch his mother's hand, her son bowed his head and heard her whisper one final "Namu Shakamuni Butsu."

6

SUTRAS ON SEX TRANSFORMATION

Eshinni's Epistle

(THIRTEENTH CENTURY C.E., ECHIGO, JAPAN)

In the summer of 2023, I was disappointed when I went to Kyoto to bow my head at the temples of Higashi Honganji and Nishi Honganji. Neither of these capacious head temples of Jodo Shinshu Buddhism had images in their worship halls of either of the women critical to the founding of their sect, Eshinni (1182–1271?) and Kakushinni (1224–1283). I feel a karmic connection to them, because the Institute of Buddhist Studies honored me to be the first steward of the Eshinni and Kakushinni Professor of Women and Buddhist Studies professorial chair I know about that is named after Buddhist women.

In an incredible historical discovery, we learned significant information about these women though ten letters the mother, Eshinni, wrote to her daughter, Kakushinni, spanning the years 1254 and 1268.[1] Eshinni, the wife of Shinran (1173–1263), the central teacher of Jodo Shinshu, wrote these letters to their daughter 650 years before they were found stored safely in a chest in Kyoto in 1921. This tantalizing discovery led me to consider the possibility of other letters we might one day find that would give us deeper insight into the thoughts and feelings of women from an earlier era. Reading Eshinni's letters helped me feel closer to her, stimulating me to reflect on what she thought about a number of sutras, including the *Lotus Sutra* and the *Larger Sutra on Amitayus*. These sutras proclaim that women must transform into male bodies to become enlightened or be reborn in the Pure Land.

I also have Eshinni consider the teachings found in two other sutras that address the relationship of bodily form to enlightenment, the *Vimalakirti Sutra* and the *Sutra on Transforming Women into Buddhas*. Her engagement with these sutras reveals her assessment of whether she thought sex transformation was required for enlightenment.[2]

Eshinni began writing these letters when she was seventy-three, after she moved from Kyoto to Echigo (present-day Niigata). Her daughter stayed in Kyoto and cared for her father. Eshinni returned to her inherited natal land. Being a landowner enabled her to support her family with the land's yield, including her husband's efforts to teach. This matriarchal tradition of women with resources supporting their husbands was still practiced during this period. Eshinni's letters are a window into this time and provide some sense of her perspective, self-awareness, concerns, and expectations. We can see the particular ways that *shinjin* (entrusting) enabled her to be strong in the face of adversity. She trusted she would receive a compassionate response to suffering as she weathered hunger and illness. She never expressed doubt. Throughout years of famines and epidemics, she focused on caring for those around her, including two orphaned grandchildren, servants who tended the land and household for her, and their families. She took her position as matriarch seriously and treated her workers as part of her extended family. Everyone struggled during these times of extreme hardship. Even while facing her own vulnerability exacerbated by her advanced age, Eshinni ensured she provided for others.

Although she was surely aware that some Buddhist teachings espoused a doctrine that only those in male bodies could be enlightened or reborn in the Pure Land, she did not betray the slightest hint that she thought being a woman was an impediment. Indeed, toward the end of her life, Eshinni conveyed in letter 10 to Kakushinni that she was confident they were both bound for rebirth in the Pure Land:

> How I wish there could be one more time for me to see you and you to see me while [I am] now in this world. I myself will be going to the [Pure Land] paradise very soon. There everything can be seen without any darkness, so be sure to say the nembutsu and come to the paradise to be with me. Indeed, when we go to the paradise and meet again, nothing whatsoever will be in darkness.[3]

Perhaps she was not unlike her husband, Shinran, who heeded the Buddhist teachings to not blindly follow but to test whether or not a teaching was effective in diminishing suffering. After two decades practicing Tendai, Shinran found the practices of that tradition were not effective for him and he decided to follow a new Buddhist leader, Honen (1133–1212), whose teachings and practices he found more helpful.

Kakushinni also demonstrated resoluteness and did not exhibit signs of feeling inferior due to her female body. Her efforts were instrumental in solidifying her father's teachings, which eventually gave rise to the establishment of the Jodo Shinshu sect (also simply called "Shin"). Ten years after Shinran's passing, Kakushinni built a memorial hall for him. Numerous followers wanted a place to go to pay their respects. Given resources and land she inherited upon the passing of her husband, she chose to ensure the hall and the property it was built on would belong to the Jodo Shinshu sangha for future generations.

Kakushinni's vision and devotion led her to establish the Ōtani Mausoleum, which gave followers a place to gather in Shinran's memory and enkindle his teachings centered on the expansive compassion of Amida Buddha, the Buddha of Infinite Light. What does Amida Buddha's compassion feel like to women who must navigate a place for themselves in a tradition that still wrestles with privileging men? The mother and daughter of Jodo Shinshu model how to navigate the landscape of life with faith, demonstrating that their female forms are not an obstacle to receiving the full force of Amida's compassion.

The legacy of the founding women apparently motivated Shin women to continue to exhibit a perspicacious understanding of Dharma. Ōtani Kinuko, a leader in the national Fujinkai—the precursor to the Federation of Buddhist Women's Associations—demonstrates this in a notable article she wrote in 1932 in which she discussed the concerns of temple wives, known as *bōmori* (guardians of the temple). Though without official status, support, or protection, bōmori worked with their ordained husbands in meeting the needs of the temple community.

Ōtani-san encouraged temple wives to "practice Buddhism,"[4] not practice Shin rules. Her advice is in direct contrast to the texts written by male leaders of the Shin administration, who stress Shin rules. Women saw a gap between Shin rules regarding women and the Dharma. Their actions tell us how their faith in Amida fueled them. Indeed, using Shinran's own logic, the more depraved a person is the more likely they will rely on Amida's compassion, and if women are more depraved than men, it stands to reason that women would more likely exhibit shinjin (trust in Amida's compassion), and, hence, be reborn in the Pure Land. That this might be so does not diminish the impact negative teachings, regulations, and institutional structures have had on people. It only makes the women subjected to inferior treatment all the more remarkable when they serve with a smile, bow with gratitude, and lead with faith.

Surely, historically and contemporaneously numerous *myōkōnin*—those heralded in Jodo Shinshu communities as exemplars of on-the-ground, everyday Buddhist faith—fill Shin temples as bōmori and lay homes as single women, wives, mothers, and daughters. Because their sincerity and humility are fundamental to their faith, they do not need recognition from anyone to receive Amida's compassion. Women may also feel Amida's compassion at work when they receive full institutional support for and official acknowledgment of their efforts and contributions. As mothers, they have raised the Jodo Shinshu community, both inside the temple and inside the home. Their intimate modeling of shinjin while they work, cook, clean, and converse with others over tea seeps into the fabric of life, infusing it with Amida's compassion. In so doing, they buoy our world with people who move with care and flow with gratitude.

Letters written by women are rich sources for learning about women's more nuanced thought. There are surely more letters and diaries that were written historically than we have access to today. The exercise of crafting a story based on historical letters invited me to imagine what a woman would think, feel, be concerned about, and hope for. Even though we will never know the full truth, understanding the sociohistorical and religiocultural context can help fortify plausibility. Moreover, the very effort to understand activates our radars and sensitivities, so we can be better equipped to discern truths and untruths when we see them.

Drawing on Eshinni's letters and my understanding of teachings and texts Eshinni might know, I imagine in the following fictionalized letter how Eshinni might think about Buddhist teachings that suggest women's bodies are categorically deficient for rebirth in the Pure Land or enlightenment. My aim is to imagine a Dharma free from such limiting views of women and their female bodies; a Dharma that, in this freedom, fully allows men and women to entrust wisdom and compassion. I imagine Eshinni would agree with this vision.

December 26, 1270
Dearest Daughter,

The winter promises to continue being harsh, so I hope you, too, are able to manage and have enough food. I am having my trusted messenger bring you some dried persimmons.

Now that I'm in my late eighties, I think it's important that I record my thoughts about being a woman. There are some passages in scriptures that had given me pause. Having deeply considered them, I have found a way they can help me, which is what sutras are meant to do: They are to teach us how to stop suffering. They are not to generate suffering. I admit that at first I was puzzled by Amida's thirty-fifth vow.

> *If, when I attain Buddhahood, women in the immeasurable and inconceivable Buddha lands of the ten directions who, having heard my Name, rejoice in faith, awaken aspiration for enlightenment, and wish to renounce womanhood should after death be reborn again as women, may I not attain perfect enlightenment.*[5]

My natural response was that Amida Buddha's compassion already supports me. Ever since your father helped me feel the mysterious depth of Amida's compassion in my life, I have rejoiced in a trusting heart. I have not, however, renounced being a woman. Perhaps my logic is simplistic, but it must be that Amida succeeded in becoming a Buddha. Therefore, as a woman, I feel safe in my sincere trust of Amida. Amida's Primal Vow affirms that compassion is for all beings who trust, and nowhere does it suggest it is limited to those with male bodies:

> *If, when I attain Buddhahood, sentient beings in the lands of the ten directions who sincerely and joyfully entrust themselves to me, desire to be born in my land, and think of me even ten times should not be born there, may I not attain perfect enlightenment.*[6]

In my mind, the eighteenth vow outweighs the ambiguous language in the thirty-fifth vow with regard to women being reborn in the Pure Land.

I have also mulled over three other sutras that include teachings about women's bodies. Like others, I found the story about a Bodhisattva doubting the Dragon Princess in the Lotus Sutra[7] *both tanta-*

lizing and open for interpretation. The young female demonstrates both her supreme understanding of Dharma and supernatural capacity to change her body at will. She uses her skills to attain Buddhahood and transform herself into a male body. Yet, this teaching occurs in a sutra well-known for teaching about skillful use of liberative techniques as acts of compassion to help people. (Remember, this is the sutra with the story about a father who uses the expedient means of "lying" to his children to get them out of a burning house.[8]) The Dragon Princess story culminates with "three thousand living beings opened up the thought of bodhi."[9] So, it seems to me she could have changed into a male form as a skillful means to help those who doubted a female, much less an eight-year-old one, could have supreme wisdom. The story highlights her magnificence. The part about turning into a male body is noted in passing. It just doesn't make sense for a path of liberation to discriminate against certain body types.

Then, I found a teaching in the Vimalakirti Sutra[10] *that gave me clarity on the matter of male and female bodies. The sutra devotes a whole chapter to a goddess instructing on the meaning and significance of nonduality. I actually found it somewhat humorous. A "goddess employed her magical power to cause the elder Shariputra [one of Buddha's disciples] to appear in her form and to cause herself to appear in his form."[11] She then delivers the Buddha's teaching: "In all things, there is neither male nor female."[12] It is nice to hear a sutra be explicit on this matter because I am tired of those with narrow and rigid thinking about women. We're sentient beings, too! We have issues, but we want to stop suffering just as much as anyone.*

Another sutra has also been clarifying. It is called the Sutra on Transforming Women into Buddhas.[13] *It proclaims, "Every woman's body: these are all the mothers of the Buddhas of the three times. Like the great sea or the great earth, for example, a woman's body is the matrix of the thus-come ones."[14] This confirms my understanding that the Buddha offered a path available to all sentient beings, including women in their female bodies.*

There is one more observation I have made that at this age I am no longer embarrassed to share with you. You know how one of the thirty-two marks of a Buddha is a sheathed lingam? It has been invoked as proof that a woman must transform into a male body in order to be a Buddha. Well maybe it's because monks who don't know any better conjured up this idea, but I think "sheathed lingam" well describes female anatomy, too.[15] *Therefore, there is no impediment to a woman or a man being a Buddha. So, I do not see how the thirty-fifth vow can be understood as an obstacle to anyone being reborn in the Pure Land.*

This is where trusting Amida's compassion has led me. I patiently wait for more people, especially men, to learn about nondual wisdom and deepen their faith in Amida's compassion. I am at peace with my interpretations. I hope you find peace, too.

7

LIBERATING HAIR

Ayamé Embroiders Her Grief

(FIFTEENTH CENTURY C.E., KYOTO, JAPAN)

I was inspired to write a story about women's hair as a vehicle of liberation. To a reader unversed in fifteenth-century Japanese Buddhist culture, that may come as a surprising idea. But Japanese Buddhist women conferred great meaning on their hair. Through their hair practices, women defied and denied claims that their bodies were polluted or unworthy of liberation. Among these women was Bifukumon'in (1117–1160). She overcame the prohibition of women entering certain areas such as mountaintop monasteries in a creative way. In her case, she wanted to benefit from the power encoded in a major monastic center on Mt. Kōya. It was, however, one of the monasteries that prohibited women from entering their grounds. Rather than acquiescing to their misogynistic rules, in 1158 she commissioned two Buddhist sculptures and, before her donations were delivered to the monastery, placed her hair inside the sculptures. In this way her body ascended the mountain.[1]

Another Buddhist practice involving hair was brought to Japan from China: the devotional and transformational Buddhist practice of hair embroidery.[2] It is a powerful and intimate practice for grieving and connecting with loved ones who have passed on—a practice almost exclusively practiced by women. Buddhist images made with women's hair are deemed sacred. Women embroidering their hair to create sacred images is their response to the ontological question raised in some Buddhist scriptures about the cleanliness of their bodies: Women's bodies are not polluted.

Most prevalent are embroideries of Amida Buddha and Kannon. The intricate and labor-intensive practice[3] was often done by wives at the passing of their husband or by daughters at the passing of their father. Embroidering with the hair of the deceased or embroidering with your own hair as you grieve a loved one is an intimate practice. In a world where the material world is understood to be animated by vital energy, embroidering Kannon with hair transforms the hair into Kannon. The embroiderer, too, is transformed by the practice. Imagine the emotions that well up and course through—sadness, longing, awareness of impermanence, gratitude, respect, love—with the thousands and thousands of stitches during the all-consuming hours, days, and months they devoted to bringing the image to life.

I invite you into my imagined story of a fifteenth-century woman, Ayamé, grieving the loss of her mother by embroidering her mother's hair into curls on Amida Buddha's head. Imagine the challenge of threading your mother's hair into the eye of a needle, tears welling up even more in the effort. Through Ayamé's experience, a palpable sense of this old Buddhist practice comes to life.

Situating the story in the reality of the Ōnin War (1467–1477), which was centered on the capital city of Kyoto, contextualizes my fictive character's loss and helps us gain a sense of the real people who lived in those times. Through the tenderness of Ayamé's relationship with her mother, we can savor the way others, too, might be moved by seeing the Mikaeri Amida Buddha statue looking back at them to see how they are. Through Ayamé bringing us to the temple where this Buddha stands, we can more readily imagine how Mikaeri Amida Buddha likely touched people during their times of fear and sadness. Through Ayamé finding a poem by the renowned Chinese poet, Su Shi (1037–1101), we can reflect on the depth of Buddhist insight that can be accessed through hair embroidery practice.

Ayamé grew up in the quiet neighborhood on the east side of Kyoto, famous for its autumn foliage of crimson red Japanese maples. It was in the environs of Eikan-dō Temple,[4] a historically renowned Jodo temple with a distinctive Amida Buddha statue. Though her family home was miraculously spared, they were horrified that the temple was decimated early in the Ōnin War. The family evermore relied on Amida Buddha for solace as they lived with vulnerability and uncertainty. Ayamé calmed herself by reliving a visit she took to the temple with her mother when she had just turned six. She still remembered how she thought the Mikaeri Amida Buddha statue at Eikan-dō looking back over his shoulder was like her mother always keeping an eye on her. That this Buddha was spared in the war confirmed her sense that Amida and her mother would care for her no matter what.

Now, though, her mother's breath was shallow. Some mysterious illness had suddenly descended upon her, sapping her life energy. She no longer wanted even a sip of water. Ayamé placed the five colored cords in her mother's hand to ensure a good passing.[5] Amida Buddha held the other end of the cords, which were attached to his hands in the *Amida Descending* (*Raigo*)[6] scroll painting hanging on the eastern wall of the room. Her mother could see Amida—attended by Kannon and Seishi Bosatsu—come down from the Western Pure Land to meet her during the time of the boar[7] on December 18, 1475. Ayamé held her mother's other hand as she breathed her last breath. It felt like proof that it was indeed the Degenerate Age of the Dharma (Mappō),[8] for her mother was struck down in her prime.

Being the eldest daughter at seventeen, Ayamé had to be strong in the face of her mother's death. Along with her father and siblings, they took turns lighting incense throughout the night. When dawn came, Ayamé cut a long lock of her mother's hair. She carefully washed the hair oil out so she could embroider it into an image of Amida. She hoped that stitching her mother's hair into the snail-shell curls of Amida's hair[9] would help her mother's rebirth in the Pure Land.[10] She chanted "Namu Amida Butsu" as she aimed to thread the needle with her mother's hair. Tears welled up, blurring her ability to see the eye of the needle. Ayamé exhaled slowly as the tears rolled down her cheeks. She continued to quietly chant "Namu Amida Butsu" and breathe slowly, letting the tears come. Eventually she threaded the needle and pierced it into the silk cloth. Her hands, breath, and lips moved in a synchronized rhythm.

The Ōnin War continued to agitate violence in the capital, deepening Ayamé's sense of pain and loss. Each time she accidentally pricked her finger, she was grateful that her mother would be safe with Amida and that she herself was alive to devote herself to the embroidery. Her sincerity was palpable through the somewhat uneven grief-stricken stitches. Ayamé offered the silk and hair image at the forty-ninth day memorial service.[11]

Ayamé noticed that the mortuary rituals anticipated the seasons of her grief. The rhythm of rituals was more frequent the first hundred days, ushering her through the most disorienting time. There were several other rituals for the remainder of that first year, climaxing with the first-year anniversary memorial service. She sensed in her bones that it would be emotionally profound, and she wanted to engage in a practice that would appropriately honor her mother and move her through this first year of grief.

In her quest, Ayamé came across a poem by the great Chinese poet, Su Shi. He wrote it as a eulogy regarding a woman who did hair embroidery practice.

> Engaging her six senses, she generates [Kannon].
> From her hand to the needle, from the needle to the thread.

How many stitches? Even a calculation expert couldn't say.
If each stitch is a Buddha, ten million Buddhas are present.
If each stitch is not a Buddha, what then can be its source?
Who has fused these two and created a gate of non-
duality?[12]

Ayamé felt a welling up in her heart. This was the depth of devotion she was seeking. Relieved that she had enough of her mother's long tresses to embroider Kannon's hair, she quivered with reverence.

An acute wave of grief rolled in as Ayamé imagined touching her mother's hair again. Embroidering her hair into Amida's curls those first weeks after her mother passed was a blur. At the time she was consumed with the aim to ensure her mother's rebirth in the Pure Land by literally sewing a part of her body to Amida. This poem now showed her a path of transforming her grief into a deepening faith. She decided to include her own hair in the image of Kannon as an expression of melting away the sense of distance that had crept in since her mother passed. In this way they would be united.

In search of a suitable fabric to embroider a Kannon on and another to wrap her collected hair in, Ayamé went into her mother's personal quarters where she had kept her embroidery materials. Ayamé first found a cream-colored silk cloth with a delicately woven pattern of clouds. She thought it would be perfect for saving her mother's midnight-black strands of long hair to embroider with. Every day, Ayamé went to comb her hair in her mother's quarters. It stirred up fond memories of her mother combing her hair for her. Ayamé carefully straightened out each strand of hair and placed it on the meter-long piece of silk fabric that her mother had saved for some future project. Each day when Ayamé folded the sides of the cloth over to protect her gathered hair, she felt her mother protecting her. Over the months she noted how the amount of hair slowly began to accumulate. She kept the cloth in which she neatly wrapped her hair on a shelf in front of the statue of Kannon her mother treasured. It was Ayamé's way of consecrating her hair before she embroidered with it.

Later Ayamé found another piece of silk among her mother's things to use for embroidering Kannon. It was in her mother's favorite color, dusty lavender. A flood of memories poured in as she mounted the cloth on her mother's embroidery frame. The embroidery frame faced the statue of Kannon on the shelf. Growing up, Ayamé always enjoyed being in her mother's personal quarters. One of her fondest activities was to sit beside her mother as they both bowed their heads to Kannon. At such times her mother's affection felt particularly tender.

Ayamé still remembered the time her mother sat in front of Kannon to explain her relationship to Amida and Kannon. It was after they returned from visiting the Mikaeri Amida when Ayamé was six. Her mother spoke with thoughtful warmth and made Ayamé feel like she had grown up enough for her mother to entrust her with something serious. Her mother shared how she relied on Amida's compassion in the same way she was assured the ground was solid under her feet and that the sun would rise and set at the beginning and end of each day. Amida was like a protective father. She turned to Kannon for more intimate and daily concerns, especially when she was worried or confused. Somehow it was easier for her to turn to Kannon, especially when she felt vulnerable and uncertain, because Kannon was female, like an understanding and wise mother.

Each time Ayamé started embroidering, she would first light incense and then bow to Kannon. Embroidering Kannon for her mother's first memorial anniversary immersed Ayamé into a deep sea of emotional and spiritual currents. Whenever there was proper light, she poured herself into this sea for hours and hours, day after day. Handling each strand of her mother's hair was both endearing and painful. Ayamé quietly chanted "Namu Kannon Riki"[13] as she threaded each strand of hair into her needle and sewed each stitch, invoking the strength of Kannon's compassion. By the time Ayamé started embroidering with her own hair, she had entered a contemplative realm, like floating in a cloud. With each stitch, Ayamé felt Kannon holding her and her mother in a warm embrace.[14]

8

CHAN MOUNTAIN SUTRA

Meihua's Wisdom Blossoms

(SEVENTEENTH CENTURY C.E., SUZHOU, CHINA)

Due to the shift in political tides generating tumult in seventeenth-century China, many women chose to become Buddhist nuns and studied, practiced, and taught Dharma. Buddha-name recitation and chanting sutras committed to memory were the core of their practice, though some also engaged with philosophically sophisticated sutras. Some trained in a nunnery before joining a small temple of four to five nuns. Others joined a small temple and remained there for the duration of their lives, though some moved to a different temple. Regardless of the size or location of where nuns practiced, they were not beholden to monk supervision. Writing poetry to express their insights into Dharma was a traditional practice among literate and classically trained nuns. Nature imagery figures prominently in their poems, indicating their refined observational skills and capacity to interpret Dharma. I was initially planning on developing my narrative around a nun who was an insightful poet. The historical record, however, already provides substantive evidence of nuns' poetry practice. Though many collections of poetry mentioned in documents are no longer available, enough of their poems remain extant to paint a picture of the richness of their minds and hearts.[1]

So, rather than centering a story on a nun writing poetry, I decided to write a story about a nun who receives a sutra after intensive meditation while on a three-year mountain retreat. The Buddhist tradition defines a sutra as the words of the Buddha. In recognition of the oral nature of the early teachings, sutras usually begin with the phrase, "Thus have I heard." Though written sutras that first appeared well after the Buddha's passing contain that phrase, too, it is easier to imagine monks are responsible for writing these sutras. The names of these likely authors are not recorded, which enhances the perception that sutras are the words of the Buddha.

Directing attention to the authorship of sutras is a way to open up reflection on the nature of sutras that are not merely written by a male but evince misogynistic views. Such sutras, or passages in sutras, are in tension with the preponderance of Buddhist teachings. The contrast beckons us to question the perspective, gender, and values of the author.

In exploring the possibility of a sutra written by a female, I was surprised to learn there are records of a few sutras that are attributed to Chinese women. Although, in keeping with sociohistorical norms, the women do not claim authorship. The earliest recorded case of a woman receiving sutras in Chinese history is of a fifth-century girl, known as Nizi, or Little Nun. She is reported to have received twenty-one sutras. During the Ming dynasty (1368–1644), Empress Dowager Li (1545–1614), mother of Emperor Wanli (r. 1573–1619), received a sutra in a dream.[2]

Another woman who received a sutra was Empress Xu (1361–1407). She records in her preface to the sutra that the Bodhisattva of Compassion, Guanyin, approached her in a dream and revealed the sutra to her.[3] The title of the sutra is the *Rarest Sutra of Great Merit Spoken by the Buddha and Received by the Empress Humane and Filial of the Great Ming in a Dream*.[4] The sutra consists of two chapters. The first chapter includes basic Mahayana teachings about the nature of mind and how we and the Buddha are no different in nature. In not realizing this, we suffer. The length of the second chapter is double the length of the first and is filled with chants, mostly dharanis—potent phrases encoded with healing and protective power—to dispel a host of dangers and to bring a myriad of blessings, giving people something they could do.[5] In her preface to the sutra, we see how she is quite a devoted Buddhist. Empress Xu writes,

> [When I was startled awake], I felt both overjoyed and filled with wonder. Trembling, I sighed and said: "This was indeed a divine dream." Quickly I fetched brush and paper and wrote down the sutra and the *dharanis* that I had received, without omitting a single word. I was aware only of an unusual flavor in my mouth and fragrant vapors and mists that lingered in my chambers for seven days without dispersing. The heavens rained down flowers for three days and then stopped, and from that moment onwards, I assiduously recited this sutra day and night without ceasing.

Later in her preface she continues, "Now I dare not keep [this sutra] secretly to myself and so I am having it carved, printed, and distributed widely so that it may serve as a ford or bridge by which people may be freed of suffering, a shortcut to the road to enlightenment. It will serve as a wide-reaching and greatly skillful means of benefit to the world."[6]

Unlike the other women who received sutras, we know quite a few details about Empress Xu, especially the concerns and values she held as expressed in her writings. Among them was her renowned conviction that women serve as moral advisors and exemplars. She promulgated and detailed this in her volume *Exhortations*, which includes twenty chapters on "Household Instructions."[7] When her son became emperor in 1409, he conferred upon his mother the title "Cultured Empress Humane and Filial, Compassionate and Virtuous, Sincere and Bright, Sedate and Devoted, Match for Heaven and Equal to the Sages."[8]

Astonished to learn of these historical examples of female recipients of sutras, I realized my idea of having a nun receive a sutra was neither daring nor a twenty-first-century progressive wish. These examples also underscored the fact that despite devoting nearly four decades to scholarly inquiry into Buddhist women, I still wasn't aware of significant portions of the available evidence of the extensive number of women with deep, strong, and visionary wisdom. They also made me wonder how much more women might have accomplished that I had never imagined.

To enter into this vibrant world of women's Buddhist practices, teachings, and wisdom insights, I created a nun, Meihua (Plum Blossom). I have her undergo training at Huideng Chan Nunnery in Suzhou, a real historical nunnery remembered for its seriousness. Through Meihua we are taken deep into the inner and outer worlds of a determined Chan nun in the seventeenth century. As she learns the teachings, we discover what nuns were taught in Chan communities. Anchoring the story in the teachings of the highly respected historical Chan Master Jizong Xingche (b. 1606) facilitates plausibility because we have records of Master Jizong's teachings, and we know she was abbess of Huideng Nunnery.[9] That she was also in the lineage of Tang dynasty Chan Master Linji Yixuan (d. 866)—whose iconoclastic approach to Chan developed into an eponymous school—breathes life into the way his approach to Chan shaped the lives and practices of Chan women.

For specific historically grounded Chan teachings and poems, I draw on Master Jizong's *Discourse Records of Chan Master Jizong Che* (*Jizong Che Chanshi Yulu*, hereafter known as simply the *Discourse Records*).[10] Having been moved by the influential teachings of a translator included in *The Biographies of Eminent Monks*, Sengzhao (384–414), she invokes them in a letter she wrote, which is recorded in her *Discourse Records*. To suggest how compelling teachings continue to be transmitted through time, in formal and informal ways, I have Sengzhao's teaching affect Meihua in a pivotal way.

To have the time frame of the story coincide with developments in the Qing dynasty that gave rise to numerous women turning to a path of Buddhist renunciation, I made Meihua's fictive teacher a disciple of the historical Master Jizong. I also introduce three of Meihua's Dharma sisters, fellow disciples of the same Buddhist teacher. After they complete their studies and training at Huideng, the four Dharma sisters launch out to form a fictive nun's temple called Purple Cloud.

In China, women mostly practiced in small groups, not as individuals. However, the most serious of Chan nuns would go off on their own for a retreat in the mountains, as exemplified by Master Jizong. Though Meihua braving the challenges of a mountain retreat is the fruit of my imagination, the location is an actual mountain—Lingyan Mountain—whose craggy cliffs tower above Suzhou.

We do not know of all the women who were inspired by Master Jizong, but it is easy to picture women being stirred by her teachings and example. Introducing fictive figures into this historical period offers a window of possibility through which to better view the strength, determination, sincerity, and spiritual accomplishments of Chan nuns and enjoy their poetic and transformative insights gained through engagements with nature.

Meihua was twenty-two when she entered Huideng Nunnery in Suzhou in 1668. Thanks to her upbringing in a gentry family, she could read. However, the family fell on hard times. Her husband died in the lingering political and social turmoil as the Qing dynasty solidified its power. The abrupt change in circumstances stirred a keen sense of the impermanence of things, and she sought deep peace. She chose the Chan nunnery due to the lingering influence of brilliant Chan Master Jizong Xingche and legendary discipline.[11] Several of the current teachers had studied under her when she was abbess for a period beginning in 1654.[12]

Meihua's teacher in the nunnery directly received the teachings of Master Jizong. In the famed Linchi lineage of the Tang dynasty, Master Jizong's teachings were undergirded by the three foci of awakening: the great root of faith, the great ball of doubt, and the great overpowering will.[13] Meihua's teacher stressed these, too, as she animated the materials in Master Jizong's *Discourse Records*, including her sermon about her path and her poetry.[14]

Meihua was inspired to learn that Master Jizong built a hut and sat in quiet meditation "from dawn to dusk."[15] Meihua was determined to do likewise someday, including doing forty-nine days and nights of investigating a *huatou*, a phrase that awakens by exhausting the possibilities of expression with speech. She was not confident, however, that she would have an authentic breakthrough as Master Jizong did.[16] To encourage herself, Meihua memorized the end of Master Jizong's sermon: "If you do not exert the strength that . . . uproots mountains, then it will be difficult to ride the ten-thousand-li black steed."[17]

Meihua also drank deeply from the pool of poems Master Jizong wrote while living in the mountains.[18] She committed one of Master Jizong's poems to memory, for it expressed what she hoped to experience someday. Meihua found reciting poetry was similar to chanting sutras. As the sound reverberated in her body, she felt it loosened debris in her heart, enabling her to experience an intimacy with the world echoed in Master Jizong's poetry:

> From the valley depths a cleansing wind rises.
> Thoughts are empty, and everything is secluded.
> One can't hear the clatter of carts and horses,
> So distant is one from the dusty cares of the world.
> When the leaves fall, we know it is autumn;
> When the trees are bare, the waterfall appears.
> Lacking all guile, the seagulls and egrets
> Become the most intimate friends.[19]

For the subtle Dharma teachings it conveyed, Meihua recited another poem over and over:

The azure sky in the window gleams pure and clear;
I open the door to let in the blue-green of the hills.
From out of the rosy mists, the lone crane returns,
Circling the rocks, then soaring up into the clouds.
A low bed of moss can be used as a meditation mat;
The scattered leaves on the eaves can serve as a robe.
The setting sun has disappeared far into the west;
The weary birds instinctively know their way home.[20]

A poem Master Jizong had written to a friend riveted Meihua with its unapologetic, dignified, and clear-minded tone:

Once you have broken through the external form of male and female,
Where in the great universe will you not find yourself totally at ease?[21]

Meihua, too, wanted to break through and be at ease. Outside of classes where Master Jizong's teachings were presented, Meihua scoured the *Discourse Records* for gems of wisdom that would help her awaken. She found one such pearl in a letter Master Jizong wrote to her brothers: "I share the same root with heaven and earth; I share the same substance with the myriad things."[22] Meihua vaguely remembered that when she first came to the nunnery eight years ago, she heard a teacher lecture on this famous Chan teaching attributed to the early Buddhist monk Sengzhao. At the time it was just a string of words to her. Now she began to feel it in her bones. She realized that studying texts was important, but that alone would not lead to awakening. This solidified her resolve to someday move beyond the shelter of the nunnery.

After completing ten years of study and practice at Huideng Nunnery, Meihua and three of her Dharma sisters set off to form their own small temple on the outskirts of Suzhou. They named their temple Purple Cloud (Ziyue-an). Because Chan nuns lived and trained in temples independent of the monks, they were aware of—but not subject to—the Garudharma rules, including the one that said, "A nun must not spend the rains in a residence where there are no monks."[23] The intention of this extra rule was to protect nuns from men who might assault them, though nuns were justifiably doubtful of its efficacy.

As these nuns settled into their temple, one day over tea they noted how they felt safer not being "protected" by a monk. All of them had heard reports of sexual abuse involving monks, so they felt safer not having a monk tasked with looking after them. Meihua intimated that one day she would like to go off by herself on a three-year retreat in the mountains, and she declared that she would feel safer alone in that setting, too. Her Dharma sisters volunteered that if any monk tried to take advantage of her seclusion and molest her, they would make sure he would be duly disciplined. Then they pretended they were adjudicating an abuse case to a sangha council and pronounced their four-part ruling to amend the suffering:

1. The monk who assaulted Meihua must meditate on a female corpse for thirty days to dissolve lust.
2. After completing the above, the assailant must meditate on a male corpse for thirty days to counterbalance any thought that there is something particularly putrid about a women's body and realize a man's body is equally putrid.
3. The assailant must gather and deliver sufficient firewood for cooking and heating at Purple Cloud Temple for five years.
4. The assailant must bow to every nun he passes for the rest of his life.

With satisfying laughter, they went to the altar to chant the afternoon sutras.

Twenty years later, Meihua decided the conditions were ripe for her to finally go deep into the mountains to live in a hut by herself for three years.[24] She wanted to go to Lingyan (Divine Cliff), the mountain that towered above their little temple. Her Dharma sisters offered to help her build a hut, but Meihua insisted on doing it by herself.

Carrying all that she could manage up the steep rocky trail, including seeds, a blanket, cup, pot, spoon, paper, ink, brush, and a cedar box for precious items—a small statue of Guanyin, sutras, and medicines—Meihua found a place to call home. There was a little spring, a clearing in the trees that was enough to let the sunshine through for vegetables to grow, and a nearby cave to retreat to for meditation. Wisteria was climbing up some rocks, and she thought it would make a nice tea. Moss blanketed a shady area near the spring, creating an inviting place to sit in meditation when the weather was mild.

Meihua decided to build her hut beside a plum tree. Not only would it provide a little shade in the summer, a plum tree would not grow so big that it would be dangerous to be near in a storm. Mostly, though, having a plum tree by her side was like having her teacher nearby. Her teacher had given her the Dharma name Plum Blossom to encourage her to be strong enough to be gentle in harsh conditions. In late winter, when snow fell on a plum blossom, her teacher never missed a chance to remind her of the wisdom of plum blossoms. Meihua was certain to have many opportunities to build strength over the next three years alone with the mountain, and the plum would be a steady reminder to approach things with patience and gratitude. She would now be tested on how deeply she had learned the various teachings.

Through a bamboo grove that blocked her hut from the wind hitting the mountain, a rock ledge opened to the south. It jutted out enough for Meihua to look to the east and west, her back to the north. From there she would sit and see sunrises and moonrises to her left and sunsets to her right. The mountain peaks across the valley stretched across the horizon. Attuning to the rhythms of the sky, she watched clouds roll through all day. With no social constructs impinging on her, she lost herself in the sea of stars by night. Meihua became friends with the beings in her midst, including the trees, rocks, and morning dew. Unmediated by language, she learned to listen to them with her whole being and felt they, too, listened to her. Whether she was in or out of harmony with the needs of the season, plants, and animals, she received direct and unfiltered feedback. Either there was sufficient food or not enough. She was thankful, too, that she had memorized her favorite sutras and poems, for they were sagacious companions during those years.

In a final push before her three years were up, Meihua was determined to do forty-nine days and forty-nine nights of meditation. On the final night, a full Harvest Moon illuminated the sky, only a few clouds on the horizon. As if the Buddha were nearby offering a sermon, she heard the voice of Dharma. Opening her eyes, an exquisite fragrance opened her heart. She grabbed her brush and wrote:

Sutra on the Liberating Senses of the Dharma Body

Guanyin attunes her senses to the music of liberation and
  purveys the world.
She hears the heartbeat of the world:
  Birds opening the morning with song,
  Water lapping on the shore,
  Cicadas swelling with undulating whirs in the summer
    heat,
  Bamboo leaves rustling in the breeze,
  Snowflakes pattering.

She sees the jewels of the world:
    Ruby sunsets,
    Silver mist dancing among the trees,
    Amber leaves falling,
    Amethyst mountain peaks,
    Golden moonrises.
She tastes the healing of the world:
    Melting ice feeding a mountain spring,
    Dewdrops quenching thirsty grass,
    Mushrooms feasting on decaying leaves,
    Crickets nibbling fiddlehead ferns,
    Bears munching berries.
She smells the beauty of the world:
    Plum blossoms peeking through falling snow,
    A cup of jasmine tea,
    Spring rain,
    Freshly tilled soil,
    Pine needles underfoot.
She touches the kindness of the world:
    Bed of moss,
    Smooth bark,
    Velvety leaf,
    Cloud shielding the full force of the summer sun,
    Warm hand.
She contemplates the cries of the world:
    Orphaned fledglings cheeping in their nest,
    A childless couple setting out food for roaming cats,
    Drought-parched crops sighing as they wilt,
    Bones of a mother fox who did not make it back to the den,
    Brush crackling in consuming flames.
As Guanyin perceives the suffering of the world,
Conducting vital energy,

Her Dharma Body responds with cosmic resonance
(*ganying*),
Harmonizing all phenomena in a symphony of liberation.

Meihua placed her sutra in the cedar box with her other valuables and then went into a deep sleep. Having accomplished her aim, she planned to return to Purple Cloud Temple when dawn broke.

Her Dharma sisters were anticipating her return. They wanted to respect her intention to be in retreat, so they remained patient. However, a month after the three-year mark, she had not arrived. It was autumn and winter sometimes arrived early. With concern weighing heavily, they finally headed up the mountain in the direction where Meihua said she would build her hut. It was an arduous climb up a rocky cliff. Along the precarious trail they found a cave halfway up the mountain. It was just big enough for them to shelter for the night. A blanket of silence wrapped them in the darkness, ruffled only by a distant rumble of thunder.

They awoke to the frantic twittering of birds rather than the melodic morning chirping. They set out with determination to find Meihua. The sun was shrouded in thick clouds, and they began to detect the smell of fire drifting through the distant trees. It had been a rather dry summer followed by a dry fall.

Fear churned in their stomachs. Trying not to panic, they forged ahead along a narrow path up the cliff, flanked from above and below by sheer rock. A vast expanse of sky exposed them to winds that cut through their robes. One of the nuns gasped when she saw what looked like a head bobbing above some rocks. As they rounded a curve, they met Meihua running toward them. The look of terror in her eyes made their hearts stop. She collapsed into their arms. After Meihua caught her breath, they all moved swiftly back down the trail.

When the smell of smoke was no longer overwhelming, Meihua explained what had happened. Out of the night sky, lightning had struck her hut, and she had soon heard flames crackling on her thatched roof. Grabbing the wooden statue of Guanyin from the little altar she had made, she placed it in her cedar box that had the sutra in it and ran out into the darkness. Her feet familiar with the trail, she could follow it even without light. She stumbled down the mountain to escape the flames that began engulfing the trees around her hut. Feeling the heat of the flames encroaching, she moved as fast as possible. The smoke would make it unsafe for her to find refuge in the cave she meditated in, but she left the box deep in the cave since she knew she would need her hands to navigate the steep rocks on the trail below. She quickly prayed the little wood box would be safe.

On the way down to Purple Cloud Temple, Meihua's Dharma sisters made her promise she would never go back up the mountain. Three years of separation instantly melted away as they affectionately expressed their deep concern for each other's well-being and punctuated their descent with teasing groans about how they were too old to be running on a craggy mountain cliff trail!

After her return to Purple Cloud Temple, Meihua would sometimes gaze up toward the mountain. At sunset the cliff took on an amethyst hue, reminding her of her healing time on the verdant peak, meditating on a soft bed of moss, smelling the fragrance of plum blossoms filling her hut, and hearing the heartbeat of the world. Over the years, the trees that had been consumed in flames gave rise to new green growth. The landscape was a sermon on impermanence, harmonizing all in a symphony of liberation.

Meihua kept her promise not to return, yet she wondered if one day someone would find the sutra treasured away inside the cave.

9

EMBODIED EXPERIENCE

Diary of a Blood Pond Sutra *Devotee*

(EIGHTEENTH CENTURY C.E., TATEYAMA, JAPAN)

The late twelfth-century Chinese apocryphal *Blood Pond Sutra* (*Ketsubonkyō* in Japanese)[1] reveals how ingenious women can be. Women in China and Japan developed strategies to navigate the beliefs instilled by the scripture, which taught that all women go to a hell pool filled with blood spilled during childbirth and menstruation.[2] Evidence suggests women who were not primary wives in medieval China found the sutra helped them in their relationships with the children they birthed. Socially, all of a man's children were considered the children of the primary wife, regardless of who the biological mother was. Therefore, in the hierarchical structure of one man having children with multiple wives, when a co-wife other than the primary wife died, her biological children had no ritual to properly grieve her because her funerary rites did not acknowledge her as a mother. The *Blood Pond Sutra* provided an impetus to change this. The sutra asserts a woman could be released from the Blood Pond Hell if her children were filial. In a Confucian-based society, encouraging filial piety supplanted the convention that sundered mothers and their children, at least in death.[3]

The *Blood Pond Sutra* began circulating in Japan during the fifteenth century. Zen priest Unrei Taizen (1752–1816) stressed women can use the sutra as a talisman.[4] The Kumano *bikuni*, or nuns of Kumano, were women who traveled significant distances in nuns' garments and offered talismans for fertility and safe childbirth for a small donation.[5] They did not necessarily join the institutionalized ordination system.[6]

I chose Mt. Tateyama in Toyama Prefecture because geographically there is a pond there designated as a "Blood Pond."[7] There is also a "Tateyama Mandala" with an "illustration of a *Ketsubonkyō* dedication service."[8] Women who died during childbirth are depicted in the Blood Pond Hell. Monks are shown throwing copies of the sutra to the women in the pond. The efficacy of this ritual is presented by women reborn on lotuses.[9]

During the Edo period, this ritual was done to ensure that women had safe and healthy childbirths. An amulet of this sutra was transformed from a source of teaching that women are condemned to a Blood Pond Hell upon death to a source of protection for pregnant women.[10] The ritual involved a woman procuring an amulet and tucking it into her obi (sash). After giving birth, the woman would remove the amulet from her sash and cut out each of the seven Sanskrit characters invoking Jizō Bodhisattva. Then, for seven evenings in a row, with a sip of water, she would swallow one tiny piece of paper with an auspicious character inscribed on it. Later she would return the remainder of the amulet to the temple whereupon she would receive a fresh copy to support her recovery from the tremendous ordeal of childbirth.[11]

The region has revived an Edo-period women's liberation ritual done before 1866, which stimulates people today to imagine women of the past in a vibrant way.[12] The geological landscape is dramatic with volcanic activity and swordlike mountain peaks. There are rust-colored ponds known as "Blood Ponds," invoking the *Blood Pond Sutra*, which, again, teaches that women are to be reborn in a Blood Pond Hell due to their parturitional and menstrual blood.[13] Rituals involving throwing copies of the sutra into such red waters were performed at numerous sites around Japan.[14] At Mt. Osorezan's Entsūji Temple, amulets of the *Ketsubonkyō* are available for people to throw into a Blood Pond on the temple grounds during a ritual performed on behalf of women who died in childbirth.[15]

Thousands of stone images produced by women's groups called Nineteenth Night consororities leave physical evidence of their activities around Japan.[16] These groups were focused on protecting women during times of vulnerability around conception, birth, and child-rearing. Though there is little preserved written documentation of the activities of these ordinary local women, these stone images are engraved with the name of their group and feature the figure of Nyoirin Kannon, a goddess particularly known for protecting women in childbirth.[17]

Japanese women also created ways to have the sutra support them and not just denigrate and oppress them. Taking cues from evidence of what practices, chants, and rituals Japanese women did—including the practices of Kumano bikuni nuns who traveled around Japan distributing teachings relating to women[18]—I narrate a story that animates how women did and can wield liberating wisdom when faced with a Buddha's words that deem their bodies a source of suffering arising from their capacity to give birth.

Our story begins in a village at the foot of Mt. Tateyama, a towering, volcanic mountain historically recognized to have a Blood Pond Hell in its environs.[19] Into this historical scenario, I have inserted a group of fictive women who live there. They come to life through passages from the imagined diary of Tora-san, who in the diary's first entry, is a newly married seventeen-year-old.

Letters and diaries written by women are rich sources for learning about women's more nuanced thought. There are surely more diaries that were written historically, but we do not have access to them today. The exercise of crafting the stories based on a diary invited me to imagine what a woman would think, feel, hope for, and be concerned about or afraid of. Understanding sociohistorical and cultural context can help fortify viable possibility, but we will never know the full truth. Trying, however, stimulates our consciousness to infer probable thoughts and emotions.

For the *Blood Pond Sutra*, we literally have "hard facts." Namely, thousands of stone markers are inscribed with "Nineteenth Night," verifying that women gathered in these spots. What we lack are "soft facts," the things women said to each other when they met and the things a woman wrote in her own diary as she processed matters of the heart relating to being a woman in eighteenth-century Japan.

Come along as we imaginatively enter this women's world of understanding, support, and historically documented creative response to a sutra that denigrates female bodies.

October 20, 1748

I went to my first gathering of the Nineteenth Night group last night. I am still shaken by the sutra we chanted. The older women there seemed unfazed by it. Afterward, some even laughed about it. How can they take it so lightly?! They clearly understand something I don't! I do seem to be behind in learning about some women's things. I guess that's not surprising since Mama died giving birth to Minami. Having helped raise my younger sister, I look forward to having children, especially since I have keen thoughts about how not to do it. Our stepmother treated us as burdens, even when we tried to help. I would not have even known about this women's gathering had my new mother-in-law not encouraged me to go.

There were about fifteen women there last night. Although I was a bit shy being introduced as the newest and youngest to join the group, I felt warmly welcomed. It was comforting to be surrounded by women who were near my age as well as women who had clearly weathered many seasons of life. Some were quiet, others were somewhat outspoken with a great sense of humor. I felt like I belonged, like the lack I felt growing up without my mother would be filled.

We did a short ritual. There was an endearing carving of Nyoirin Kannon on a low table at the front of the room. The women rotate who is to bring flowers and food offerings. One of the older women lit a can-

dle and incense. Another woman rang a bell, indicating when to bow. After three bows, we chanted the Heart Sutra. *Like most people, I could chant it by memory. Then they began to chant a sutra I had never heard before. Why were women in hell wallowing in a pond full of menstrual blood?! And forced to drink it!!! Beaten with an iron rod if they refused?! Wasn't a sutra supposed to be the words of an enlightened being? What is going on?! The part about washing out our monthly cloths polluting the water tea is made with is infuriating because women are very careful about such things! A man must have written this!*

The ritual ended with prayers. Some prayed to get pregnant. Others prayed for a safe birth for their baby and themselves. Women added prayers for sisters and friends who were not there, some because they were caring for sick children.[20] *After the personal prayers, the women intoned a formal prayer in unison that paraphrased the earlier sutra: "May all women be released from the Blood Pond Hell and reborn in the Buddha's Land."*[21]

Most of the evening was spent sharing stories. One elder woman—who seemed to be a special visitor—guided us by weaving wisdom into her tale of affliction and adversity.[22] *The night drew to a close with a bell and a bow.*

As I was walking out, a middle-aged woman came over to welcome me. She had an especially warm smile and a sparkle in her eyes. Her name was Kané-san. I immediately sensed her care. She is how I imagine Mama would be if she were still around. I miss her.

November 20, 1748

It's hard to believe one month has already passed. During casual conversation over tea, I felt like I was being initiated into a woman's world of unvarnished honesty and humor. When one young woman complained about her cramps, a refreshingly salty woman named Kuma-san exclaimed, "That's why we don't have to do certain rituals and such when it's our time of the month! Men think they're controlling us because we're polluted, but really it's because they're afraid of blood. They have no idea that their rules are really giving us a break when we need it most! Besides, who wants to move around a lot and risk soiling our clothes? There's enough laundry as it is!!" Kané-san even chimed in, saying she thought these rules were humane because they gave women time to rest and be restored by having a respite to reflect.

These women's gatherings are fantastic!!

January 20, 1749

More than a month has passed since . . . this is the first time it's happened. I'm usually so regular. I guess we have been married for four months, but I didn't know it would happen this fast. So, it must be . . . Before going to the gathering, I was a tumult of emotions. I was excited about becoming a mother, but fear of dying like Mama felt like a typhoon roaring through me. I was practically paralyzed with the thought that . . . I can't even say it . . . that a storm would return my baby to the waters. . . . My best friend is still struggling to get up and prepare food after that happened to hers.

When I shared this at the gathering, I could feel the fear of dying in childbirth ripple through the circle of women.[23] *Tomi-san chanted "Namu Amida Butsu" under her breath. Kané-san walked over to me, held my hands, and looked deeply into my eyes. "You are not alone, Tora-san. We are here for you." As we chanted the* Blood Pond Sutra *together, instead of being repulsed by it, I felt embraced in a wave of understanding. Their voices bathed me in compassion. They all prayed for me with a sincerity that made me feel it would be alright.*

February 20, 1749

Kané-san gave me an amulet to protect me through pregnancy and delivery. She had traveled a great distance to a Kumano bikuni, a kind of Buddhist nun known for understanding the types of suffering women face. It turns out it was the elder woman who had shared a powerful story that first night I joined the gathering. Kané-san trusted this nun, so she wanted to get the special Blood Pond Sutra *amulet from her. There are many Kumano bikuni who travel around the Kii Peninsula supporting women with teachings and these special amulets.*

I peeked inside the cloth amulet and found a copy of the Blood Pond Sutra *written on very thin paper.*

May 20, 1749

My belly has suddenly swelled, throwing off my balance. I've learned that means things are progressing on schedule. Kané-san knew how to wrap the long cotton sash, a haraobi, just tight enough to support my growing belly and relieve the strain on my lower back. She tucked the amulet she had given me in between the folds of the obi so it would stay close to my body. I felt protected and had less back pain.

August 10, 1749

My daughter, Hatsu, was born. We are both safe! The Blood Pond Sutra *amulet works! Of course, the women and their prayers saw me through, too!*

October 18, 1755

I have been so busy raising my children, I have not had time to write. Today, though, I must write.

We all gathered for Tomi-san's funeral. She died in childbirth. I carried a small statue of Nyoirin Kannon to place on a large flat rock we used as an altar at the edge of the Blood Pond.[24] *Others brought food offerings that, as the sutra prescribed, we would later feast on. We came to this desolate place on the craggy mountain for funerals.*

The aroma of sulfur cast a solemn pall over us. The sutra assures liberation for those who "hold a Blood Pond Liberation service,"[25] *which includes chanting the sutra and doing a secret ritual shared among women. We took a quiet moment at the edge of the pond. In silence, we each reverently held a Blood Pond amulet to our bowed foreheads. The amulets rent the pond as we threw them in to set free our prayers for Tomi-san. Then, as the sutra instructs, we placed a copy of the sutra into a boat and set it afloat in the pond.*[26] *The sutra promises that after doing so "a five-colored lotus flower would appear in the middle of the Blood Pond."*[27]

As the sun sank lower on the horizon, a few women went with me to place the Nyoirin Kannon on Tomi-san's grave. I have come to trust that women would not be condemned to the Blood Pond Hell.[28] *I believe the sutra not only assures safe births, but that if a woman did die in childbirth, she would be reborn in the Pure Land.*[29]

May 24, 1756

Eight days ago, I gave birth to my fourth child. Tomi-san was on my mind. My father-in-law gave my son the name Kennosuke. As with my other three babies, for the first seven nights, I did the ritual to invoke Jizō Bodhisattva's protection. It's especially helpful while recovering from delivery. From the Blood Pond amulet, I removed the paper on which the seven Sanskrit syllables for Jizō's dharani are written: "On-ka-ka-kabi-san-man-e." Each night, I carefully tear off one Sanskrit syllable and swallow it with some water. For extra protection, I also whisper the Heart Sutra.

Today I went to the temple to receive a fresh copy of the sutra and return the one that had served me. I always feel comforted keeping the sutra close to my body, especially until I am fully restored from the birth.[30]

It seems like a lifetime ago when I was disturbed by this sutra. Now I see that the sutra brings women together. When we gather, we naturally support each other. This is what makes the sutra so powerful. I don't know how I would have survived without my Nineteenth Night group!

June 2, 1757

My younger sister, Minami, gave birth to her first child today. They are both safe! I'm sure the amulet helped. When the time comes, I will give one to her daughter, too.

10

EARTHQUAKE AND WAR

Grandma's Healing Home

(TWENTIETH CENTURY C.E., TOKYO, JAPAN)

Over the course of nearly fifteen centuries of Japanese culture being transformed by and transforming the Buddhist tradition, Buddhist values and principles have become thoroughly integrated into mundane activities and common ways of thinking and speaking. It is easy to miss the power of these teachings, especially when they are seen as ordinary, routine, and natural. People are often not conscious that they are engaging Dharma.[1] For instance, a Japanese mother is often a child's first Buddhist teacher, even if she is not intentionally trying to transmit Dharma. Mothers, however, rarely receive acknowledgment for being a person's first Buddhist teacher. Nonetheless, as they respond to familial needs on a daily basis or in a crisis, many women have become adept at wielding the liberating power of Dharma.

This was the case with my mother. She did not think in terms of nor use Buddhist terms. She taught me Dharma by the way she expected me to behave. As an expression of gratitude for all who provided the conditions for my life, I was to work hard and not give up. It was easy to feel grateful, for I did not suffer like she had. As I mentioned in the opening, she was born three weeks before the 1923 earthquake in which her father's legs were profoundly injured in his effort to save her. This injury plunged the family into poverty. Although

I could not imagine the terror of it, she also lived through bombings and beatings during World War II–era Japan. Having survived these events, she did not become bitter and resentful. She even married "the enemy," my white father from Detroit. She was determined to raise me to recognize how my actions and expressions affected others, to not be self-centered, and to be honest and kind. Now I can see those were lessons in interdependence and no-separate-self, the undergirding reason it is wise to be compassionate.

In a way, for many, one's first sangha is the family in which one is raised. Whoever it might include, the whole family is involved in shaping a child's world. It is not unusual for a child to first taste the prime causes of suffering—delusion, desire, and hatred—in the dynamics of a family facing the sociopolitical and economic conditions of their times.

In Japan, a home altar provides many families with a space to remind them that there are options in the way one responds to life's challenges. Altars are often centered on memorial rituals for deceased loved ones. Many Japanese Buddhist sects have come to refer to a deceased family member as a Buddha upon their passing. I call such a Buddha a "Personal Buddha,"[2] for families engage with them as a wise, compassionate, and understanding being who looks after the family. In this manner, Japanese familial relationships connect life and death, extending the network of support a family can rely on. Ritually maintaining multigenerational connections often fortifies family members to integrate losses in ways that affirm and strengthen. In these ways, Buddhist modes of being are infused into the foundation of everyday life and a home becomes a refuge for healing.

I want to underscore Dharma activities and lessons in the home because I want people to notice those wielding the liberating power of Dharma in daily life. Many of these people are women and are little recognized. I also want to free people from or expand upon the notion that the monastic mode is the only serious form of Buddhist practice.

A monastic-inspired mode of centering on meditation practice predominates among first-generation lay Buddhists in the West because cultivating a culturally attuned mode of Buddhist practice in the home often takes more than one, if not many, generations. Many first-generation Buddhist families struggle with scheduling and addressing all family members' needs when Buddhist practice is primarily focused on seated meditation. Seated meditation is powerful, but it is not the only Buddhist practice that is powerful. Numerous Buddhist practices, especially those focused on serving others and cultivating moral ways to concretely respond to suffering in one's midst, are vital to integrate into the dynamics of home life. I have heard many first-generation Buddhists, mostly women, suffer from anxiety that they don't have enough time to practice because "practice" is understood to happen on the meditation cushion. The gendered differential in complaints regarding lack of time to "practice" seems to arise out of gendered expectations of domestic and childcare responsibilities. A shift in understanding "practice" can help resolve some of the anxiety and tension, though a full resolution lies beyond the scope of this book. Cultivating intuition about how to integrate Buddhist "practice" into home life will take more generations of people adapting it into their own cultural context, but we can learn from the ways multigenerational Buddhist families weave Buddhist teachings into their lives. I wrote the following story to help usher that process along and to convey that Dharma in the home can be deep enough to hold profound grief and strong enough to liberate people from hate.

Though we have documentation for many people in twentieth-century Japan, we do not have detailed records of what the average mother and grandmother thought and taught to their children and families. This story, deliberately set during the great earthquake of 1923 and World War II, enables us to consider how women in the home helped their families survive and heal from major life tragedies. The dates of events—earthquake, bombings, and soldier deployment and return—are historically accurate. With one exception, the locations and their names are historically documented and include Tokyo Senmon Gakkō,[3] Ōkuma Garden, three locations in Asakusa—Sensōji Temple,

Daikokuya Tempura restaurant, and Ryōunkaku—Higashi-Nihonbashi, the Sumida River, Pearl Harbor, the southwestern Pacific Ocean island of New Britain, Rabaul, Hiroshima, and Nagasaki. The ritual practices, ritualized words, and common phrases described in the story are all authentic.

To this history, I bring to life the friends and members of a fictional three-generation family that runs a fictitious soba shop, Waraku (Enjoy Together). The Ishikawa family includes Obāchan (Grandma), Ojīchan (Grandpa), their adult son Isamu, their daughter-in-law Emiko, and their grandson Kazuki.

The daily rhythm of life for the Ishikawa family was governed by the needs of running their soba shop, Waraku. Since it was located near Tokyo Senmon Gakkō university (renamed Waseda University in 1902), they had a steady stream of students, especially at lunch. Obāchan and Ojīchan opened the soba shop shortly after they were married in 1892. The university had been established ten years earlier. They thought being near the campus would be a promising location, though it was a quieter area. They lived in a house attached to the shop and in time had children who grew up and went off to start their own families. Their eldest son, Isamu, stayed home to help run the soba shop, and he married Emiko in 1920. Life was stable and cheerful.

In 1922, two wonderful things happened: Their first grandchild, Kazuki, was born, and the nearby Ōkuma Garden was donated to Waseda University. This brought more business to their soba shop just as the needs of the family were increasing. In addition to students, those wanting to stroll through the gardens would make it a nice outing by stopping for a meal at Waraku.

One Saturday, Ojīchan went to Asakusa with an old friend who wanted to go to Sensōji, an ancient and powerful temple, to pray to Kannon for his aging mother. She had caught a cold that not only was not clearing up but seemed to be getting worse. After offering incense, they waved the smoke over their bodies, especially their heads and hearts. They wanted to transport the healing blessings to their families. They went up to the main altar, threw coins in the offering box, and bowed their heads for an extended time. Then they left the temple, walked back down the steps, turned right, and happily decided it was time for lunch. It was a treat for them to eat out, and they had heard of a place called Daikokuya Tempura that was renowned for its *tendon*.[4]

As they walked around looking for the restaurant, they saw the towering Ryōunkaku (Cloud-Surpassing Pavilion).[5] At twelve stories high, it had a commanding presence, and it felt festive in the midst of the bustling crowd. Since running a restaurant seldom allowed Ojīchan time for sightseeing, they decided to take advantage of the opportunity to go see the building before eating lunch.

But as they started toward it, the earth beneath their feet suddenly began to shake and roar—an earthquake! Ojīchan and his friend were knocked off balance, and the soaring tower began to fracture, its pieces crumbling to the ground all around them. People shrieked and ran for cover as panic set in. When it was over, one hundred and forty thousand people, Ojīchan and his friend among them, had perished in what became known as the Great Kanto Earthquake on September 1, 1923. Obāchan was made a widow at forty-nine.

Because she was not alone in her tragic loss, Obāchan did not succumb to self-pity, though grief flooded her and everyone else in the family with sorrow. They all still interacted with Ojīchan at their home altar. His photo and the mortuary tablet (*ihai*) that had his Buddhist name engraved on it were placed inside the altar. Death can dissolve delusions, so upon passing, a loved one is recognized as a "Personal Buddha," an enlightened being who deeply understands and clearly sees you.

Persimmons were one of Ojīchan's favorite fruits, so when they ripened later that fall, they offered him some on the altar and ate their own as a family at a low table nearby. It felt like Ojīchan was there.

Although Kazuki was only a year old when Ojīchan passed, he grew up having regular casual conversations with him as part of the family. All important milestones were shared with Ojīchan, such as when Kazuki began to talk, started school, and learned to ride a bike. Kazuki knew Ojīchan's favorite foods and always offered them to him first on the altar. Kazuki felt Ojīchan caring for him. He felt connected and protected. Though no one told him directly, Kazuki learned in his bones that death was not the end of a relationship. Indeed, he never thought otherwise, because the continued connection was all he ever knew.

The home altar was an anchor for the heart of the family. It helped them to stay moored when life did not go as hoped. The family consulted Ojīchan on matters of importance or those that caused anxiety, for he was the fount of wisdom in the family. When requesting encouragement from Ojīchan, one could practically hear him intone the motto, SEVEN TIMES DOWN, EIGHT TIMES UP.[6] It was his favorite mantra, and he never tired of using it to encourage people to get up and continue on, even after falling down seven times. He proclaimed, as long as you are alive, you can get up. Even in death, he spurred people to rise and go on.

Meals were a time for nourishing both the body and heart. Kazuki grew up with the family putting their hands together in prayer, bowing, and saying *itadakimasu*[7] before eating. Gratitude was a staple, and it was always expressed with a bow. Being grateful meant to be consciously aware of all the beings—including the sun, rain, and soil—that contributed to the food on their table. The care of farmers bending their backs for hours and hours, days upon days, to plant and tend the rice, buckwheat, daikon, cucumbers, eggplants, *satsumaimo*, soybeans, and kabocha were all, in a sense, at the table. If Kazuki expressed dislike for some food by eating around it and leaving the unfavored item in his bowl, somebody at the table, most often his Obāchan, would say, *Suki kirai wa dame*, which meant, "It's bad to favor or dislike."

This one bit of advice required Kazuki to cultivate patience, to not just think about himself, and to respect others who supported him—even those he could not actually see. Growing up repeatedly hearing that it was bad to favor or dislike eventually led him to a deeper understanding of how he was part of an interrelated web of relationships. His feelings, choices, and actions affected others. He came to realize that it was not that he didn't matter, but that others mattered, too. He could not survive, much less exist, were it not for the help of others. No one ever talked about these things as Buddhist teachings.

Kazuki was nineteen when Japan bombed Pearl Harbor, escalating the war ravaging the world. In search of the meaning of life, he read a short introductory book on Buddhist teachings. He was surprised to learn that the admonition to not favor or dislike steered him away from two of the three poisons that generate suffering: greed and hatred. The constant reminders to be respectful and grateful for others hedged him away from the third poison, delusion, especially the root delusion of being a separate self.

He asked his mom if she was trying to teach him to be Buddhist, but she said she was not. She was just trying to raise him to be respectful and grateful. The book never mentioned Buddhist altars in the home, so Kazuki asked if their altar made them Buddhist. His mom responded, "I never thought of it that way. It's just the way we respect and let Ojīchan know we are grateful for him."

Kazuki felt a tension between how he was raised and the social currents pressing people to be respectful to the emperor of Japan by supporting the war and being grateful for the military acting bravely in Japan's interests.

One day, the letter the family had dreaded arrived, conscripting Kazuki into the war on April 10, 1942.[8] Every morning thereafter, Obāchan asked Ojīchan to watch over their grandson. Kazuki was sent to a major strategic Japanese hub on the Pacific island of New Britain.[9] Later, the family received a letter from him letting them know he was in the town of Rabaul. They sensed he was putting up a brave front, but they knew he was morally conflicted. He was learning firsthand the wisdom of Ojīchan's motto, though he sometimes wondered, *Rise for what?*

Snow covered Tokyo on Sunday, February 25, 1945. The city appeared practically pastoral. Isamu decided to check on an old classmate who he heard was struggling. His two sons, born eleven months apart, had gone to war and would never come back. He sent his wife and daughter to the countryside to be with his wife's sister on a farm where they might be safe and get enough food. Isamu brought rare treats he got on the black market: coffee and sugar. The hour it took him to ride his bicycle across Tokyo was dismal because this once thriving metropolis was drained of food; rations were not enough to fill one's belly.

As he approached his friend's house near the Sumida River, just beyond Higashi-Nihonbashi, he remembered fun times they had growing up. They had been best buddies. His friend had moved across town for a job after finishing his schooling, so they didn't see each other often. Isamu was lost in thought, feeling nostalgic for those carefree days, when out of nowhere a B-29 bomber appeared over his head and dropped its bombs.[10] His wife, Emiko, became a widow at age forty-five.

Obāchan knew how to be there for Emiko after losing her husband, but she did not know how to be with herself after outliving her son. She was numb. Both of them were numb. SEVEN TIMES DOWN, EIGHT TIMES UP rang hollow. The war had ripped their hearts out. Although they had miraculously survived the firebombing raid that desecrated Tokyo, it and the atomic bombs that obliterated Hiroshima and Nagasaki were incomprehensible. Their fear and love for Kazuki were the only things that kept them going.

When the war was declared over on September 2, 1945, they thought the hell they had been enduring over the past six months had ended. They thought no news about Kazuki was good news, but still they could not exhale. They rose every morning and prayed to Ojīchan and Isamu that today would be the day Kazuki came home from the war. Autumn foliage fell. No Kazuki. Snow fell. No Kazuki. Spring flowers bloomed. No Kazuki.

On May 26, 1946, 266 days after the war had ended—each day suspended in an eternal limbo of hope and agony—Kazuki came home.

The three of them sobbed cathartic tears as they lit incense and thanked Ojīchan and Papa (Isamu) for protecting Kazuki. Kazuki, however, was a ghost of the young man who went to war over four years earlier. He could not unsee or unhear the horrors he had lived through. Even though being home was a relief, he doubted he had any purpose for existing.

Kazuki went through the motions of getting up and helping out. He repaired damage the soba shop and house sustained during the war. As the months passed, Kazuki began to hear Ojīchan whisper in his ear, "SEVEN TIMES DOWN, EIGHT TIMES UP." Kazuki started repeating it under his breath as he went through the day finding things to repair and neighbors to help. It was now his mantra. Despite not having clarity about the value of getting up, he trusted Ojīchan would not lead him astray. So, he kept getting up and matter-of-factly doing what was needed in the moment. He felt ashamed that he did not feel gratitude for being alive or for his beloved Obāchan's and mother's survival when hundreds of thousands had been killed, including his own father.

Finally, in a quiet conversation on the *engawa*,[11] Kazuki opened up and confessed to Obāchan that during the war he had learned to hate. Obāchan, too, had to confront the hatred that had burned in her heart after Kazuki's father, her eldest son, Isamu, was killed. The hatred consumed all the light in her world. She was angry at everything, including Ojīchan for not protecting their son from harm. Even though she had survived night after night of firebombings, she, too, had no sense of gratitude.

Kazuki's mom joined them on the engawa. She confessed that she also had to wrestle with the hatred that was burning her up from the inside out, especially after her husband was killed by an indiscriminate bomb. They sat in silence and let the tears come. None of them had cried over the losses of the war until now. Through the long war, they had each been held in suspended animation, afraid to live.

Obāchan broke the silence with a thunderous proclamation that erupted from the depths of her being: "There are no enemies!" She gasped as if the commanding voice came from someone else. The armor she had shielded her heart with cracked open. Her voice rumbled with determination as a part of her old self buried under the rubble of war rose up. "Suki kirai wa dame. It's bad to favor or dislike, whether it's vegetables or people. Suki kirai wa dame!"

Exhaling audibly, Kazuki's mom got up to cut some persimmons. Kazuki offered some to Ojīchan and Papa first. They sat together and savored the flavor of autumn. Sighing, Obāchan gazed beyond the treetops where the sunset had painted the sky in soft pinks and purples. It probably had done so countless times in the past years, but she had not looked up to see. She motioned with her head for the others to look up, too. Gratitude began to trickle into their aching but healing hearts.

PART TWO

Dharma Women Blossoming in the Present

ETHNOGRAPHIC PORTRAITS

In the previous stories, women's methods of liberating Dharma from narrow views were illuminated in a variety of sociohistorical settings and phases of the tradition. In the following nonfiction vignettes, I draw on conversations with Buddhist women currently living in the West. I wondered how women around me applied Dharma to the challenges of twenty-first-century America. I sought the counsel of several women I knew to be serious practitioners of the Buddhist path. Their heartbreaking and heart-inspiring stories made clear that they drank as deeply from the well of Dharma as did women who lived in sociocultural contexts that were shaped by a centuries-long engagement with the Buddhist tradition.

Each woman I spoke with had cultivated a wealth of insight and wisdom, often born from experiences of suffering. Those who generously and courageously shared their perspectives and opened up about their intimate and painful experiences range in age from sixty-four to seventy-five. They include "Euro-white" and Japanese American racial ethnicities, hetero- and homosexual orientations, and college and graduate school educational levels.

Most are native English speakers, though a few know some Japanese. Some are first-generation Buddhists, and others come from multigenerational Buddhist families. They include those committed to Soto Zen and Jodo Shinshu, as well as those who weave in other traditions. Both lay and ordained people are represented. Some of these women gave birth to and raised children, and others parented children they did not birth. The types of work they have done range from governmental and high tech to scientific research and social work.

To respect the privacy of the women who shared their stories with me, I obfuscated some personal identifying information in the stories. All names are pseudonyms. Collectively, these stories gathered during the summer of 2024 offer a select view of Dharma activity in the San Francisco Bay area, a significant cultural arena for Buddhism in the United States, as the country's first Buddhist temple was built in San Francisco in 1853.[1]

Through these stories we can see multiple ways women wield liberating power in the contemporary Buddhist landscape of the United States, revealing how perennial certain kinds of challenges are as well as how particular sociopolitical conditions give rise to resilience, creativity, and wisdom.

11

POISON OF PATRIARCHY

(TWENTY-FIRST CENTURY C.E., UNITED STATES)

With deep respect for the way Rebecca carries herself, I was drawn to hear what helped her cultivate such balanced and patient perception in the face of notable gender discrimination. Out of concern to help other women, she openly shared moments of vulnerability and frustration and how Dharma helped her navigate tense and disempowering experiences. Though a highly respected senior teacher who received Dharma transmission over a decade ago, Rebecca finds being a woman makes it a struggle to be seen.

Zen Master Dogen's work *Shobogenzo* is one of Rebecca's primary teachers. This thirteenth-century text cuts through the centuries to illuminate the capacity of each being to manifest Buddha-nature in daily life. He instructs that we have a choice each moment to be respectful and caring or not. For all his philosophically subtle and penetrating writings, Dogen was a profoundly concerned teacher. He devoted himself to helping people wake up from unnecessary suffering.

Therefore, Rebecca relies on his magnum opus as a confidant in times of profound grief and struggle. She turns to it for guidance in the ways of finding peace in the face of impermanence. For Rebecca, it is a steady source of wisdom free of the toxic dynamics that often accompany communities full of people who are tired of suffering. Seeking relief requires facing the root causes of suffering, which are always some permutations of delusion, attachment, or aversion. Being active in such a community offers ample opportunities to practice patience, listen to the cries of the world, and be compassionate to self and others.

Rebecca reflects on meetings with ordained Buddhist men, especially when she is the lone woman. Men will look each other in the eyes and avoid hers. When she contributes a point, it is as if her voice is not heard. Though her idea is not acknowledged, when a man later makes the same point, other men think it's a good idea. She observes how these are some of the quietly insidious ways patriarchy manifests. Such dynamics are generally disheartening for women in society. In a community of people who have vowed to follow Dharma, it is painful.

With dignity and open-eyed awareness of the challenges, Rebecca appreciates that everyone in the Dharma community agrees with the tenets of equality. Everyone has Buddha-nature. Everyone can actualize enlightenment. Equality is proclaimed. She knows, too, that human interactions do not always bring these teachings to life. Many men can't even see how patriarchal behaviors are woven into the fabric of their habits. She finds it agonizingly ironic that invocations of equality seem to make it harder for men to see themselves clearly, that patriarchy is a privileged position. Rebecca recognizes that something pernicious is going on.

She discerns that patriarchy is itself an intoxicant. As a teacher, she is keenly attuned to how practice offers the precepts as guides to upright behavior. The fifth precept reminds us to not intoxicate body or mind of self or others to proceed clearly. For Rebecca, unexamined patriarchal behavior equates to intoxicating body or mind.

Because of Rebecca's professional experiences as an addiction counselor, she often thinks about the Dharma and the path of recovery, finding numerous parallels. In so doing she finds some common markers of dysfunction. Among the hallmarks of addiction are denial and secrecy. Similarly, denying inequities that arise because of gender differences or keeping inappropriate patriarchal behaviors secret can sadly, to this day, be found in active and even well-intentioned practice centers.

"Honestly," Rebecca says, shaking her head sadly, "to this day, people, practitioners, come to me, even some in positions of Dharma authority. They come to me in hushed whispers. Not too long ago I heard from a woman member of a prominent Midwestern practice center where several women were directly instructed not to talk about the disparity of treatment and opportunity they felt due to gender. Pretty incredible."

With insight gained from her professional training, Rebecca knows you can't embody the wisdom of the Buddhist tradition unless you have clarity—clarity of heart, mind, and body. Without clarity, you cannot access the healing depths of Buddhist wisdom.

Rebecca is careful to acknowledge there is some biology that predisposes people to turn to substances and addictive behaviors. Turning to intoxicants is not only caused by the karmic crucible in which people grow up. Feeling you're not good enough may sound like a trite characteristic, but it has devastating consequences. Those biologically predisposed often water toxic seeds out of ignorance. That's part of addictive behavior. You swear you'll never do *X* and then take it on and water it. Recovery teaches you that you can transform suffering. With Dharma, we get to take that into another paradigm of transformation. Yet those who are in recovery have a leg up. You have confidence you can take on this suffering because you have already done it. You've been through a major Dharma gate.

Any intoxicant can cloud our vision, obscuring its full and harmful impact and often occluding our own role in perpetuating it. This is true for patriarchy as well: "Everyone is vulnerable to the intoxicant of patriarchy," Rebecca says, "no matter where they fall in gender. We all need to wake up, take a clear look, take responsibility for our part, and then embody a different way forward, a liberative way forward. Dogen spells it out quite clearly in 'Receiving the Marrow.' He says, 'Do not discriminate between men and women. This is the most wondrous principle of the Buddha way.'"

Rebecca remembers a client pointing out that recovery is not necessarily a hotbed of mental health. She notes that it is the same with Zen: "We're all working on it as best we can. May we all proceed clearly."

Through it all, Dogen is by her side guiding her to expand her perception, deepen her understanding, and strengthen her magnanimity as she lives and teaches in these conditions.

12

BUDDHA WAS ASLEEP IN OUR HOME

(TWENTY-FIRST CENTURY, C.E., UNITED STATES)

Sunlight streamed through the Douglas fir branches as Saya and I sat at her walnut kitchen table. Saya has a warmth and gentleness that drew me in. Having weathered seven decades, I knew her story would include times of struggle. I surmised that due to her Japanese American heritage her family suffered the blatant racism and wartime incarceration, a communal suffering that stained the US Constitution. Given her graciousness, I wondered what other personal trials had polished her kind heart.

Saya leaned forward and looked squarely into my eyes. The gravity of sacred time and space pulled us closer as she began: "I have never told anyone this before. I was in my twenties. I had an abortion."

For over fifty years, only her partner knew. He accompanied her across state lines to receive the procedure, since it wasn't available in the state they lived in. He cared for her afterward, too. It was a mutual decision. They weren't ready to responsibly parent.

"We did not regret our decision," Saya says. "Yet, there's not a day that goes by that I don't think about it. It's not that I feel shame, but it is so personal. Something unresolved lingers in me. There's a dialogue inside me. There was a longing to connect, but

I didn't know how. I decided to share this because of the times we live in now. So many women are suffering. Girls who are raped must carry a baby, and they don't know what is going on with their bodies. Women with complications in pregnancy die because doctors fearing jail wait until they do not hear a heartbeat before they will treat a woman. Since many will read your book, I wanted to share how Dharma helped me in ways that I am only now learning how to articulate. It had been so deeply embedded in daily life that I didn't have words to understand it, but I realize now that it has undergirded my whole life.

"My family did not do explicit rituals or have Buddhist images. They came to the United States in the early 1900s. When they came from Japan, they did not know what to expect. They feared that having explicit Buddhist items might subject them to adverse treatment, so they did not bring them. They did know that they did not look like the anglicized depictions of Jesus or Mary. They did not know that coming to this land to till fields and grow vegetables would become a threat to white Americans. Rounded up into internment camps, they were forcibly detained behind barbed wire on land that was not arable.

"Our family was one of the fortunate ones, for a white man looked after our family farm and returned it to us when my family was freed. I was born not long after that. My mom was quite young, so my Obāchan pretty much raised me. Living on a farm, we always had a lot of food and there was always a lot of sharing. Aunties, uncles, cousins, and neighboring farm families were my world.

"My Obāchan was Buddhist, so I knew I grew up culturally Buddhist. It recently became clear to me that I had actually been raised in the Dharma. I was living it but not knowing it. It was just the way things were done. I see now that Obāchan taught me by how she carried herself, how she lived her ethics. She expected me to, as well. The qualities she embodied included honesty, hard work, reliability, integrity, generosity, standing tall, being a 'good person' and being kind.

"I learned *gaman*—a kind of patience or forbearance—from my Obāchan. She came to this country with harsh conditions. Gaman got her through dark times, including the war and incarceration. Gaman enabled her to make lemonade out of lemons. Gaman doesn't translate well into English because it's not based on an individualistic sense of self. Awareness of our dependence on each other is implicit in gaman. Being patient or exhibiting fortitude is experienced as being an important part of a larger whole, which is integral to a relational notion of self. You are not alone. And you are not doing things just for yourself. Your actions affect others. So when you endure a difficult situation, you are enacting your respect and care for the greater whole.

"I have learned that gaman is a mature response to not getting what you want. Gaman is an antidote to self-pity. It is not about self-denial but about understanding there are limitations to conditions and resources. Gaman is a patience that stretches you. It is founded on a network of support. You do not have to have concrete knowledge of the past to draw on ancestral strength and wisdom because it is baked into current conditions. Gaman is also an expression of respect for conditions of the present and awareness that consequences of one's actions ripple out into the future. Gaman is driven by a sense of gratitude for what you have received and moral responsibility for those who will be affected by your choices. Gaman has helped me see things from a bigger perspective, to know that I am not alone in my times of forbearance. It makes it easier to regulate my emotions as they course through me.

"I have come to appreciate how growing up in a farming family kept me close to nature and community. I learned the cycle of life and death growing up on a farm among all my cousins, aunties, and uncles. We were there for each other through births, holidays, sicknesses, and deaths. The transformation of seasons was also a teacher that gave instruction through changes in temperature, sunlight, rain, wind, and soil, through tiny sprouts and harvested vegetables. To this day, gardening keeps me in touch with the natural dynamics of reality. That's how I approach things. It guides how I process emotions. Nature flows with birth and death, and I am part of that. It makes me want to have my hands in the soil. The growing and planting season is important to me. It's the nurturing, the concern if the little young ones will make it. Others can handle the harvest. I want to care for the vulnerable seedlings and insects. I watch the interactions of insects moving around in the flowers. They show me how all things are interconnected.

"This view of the circle of life fortified me as I cared for my aging father. He was the oldest of four sons. They all worked the farm together. After he got sick, they pressured him to retire early. Farming was his whole world, his identity. So to not work was devastating for him. Although he adored his children, he had anger issues. Since I was the eldest in my generation, my mom raised me to set a good example for my younger siblings and cousins. I had to be sure to not behave in any way that was disrespectful because the younger ones would see what I did. I would set the standard. Moreover, what I did would reflect on everyone. I had pressure to keep our family name upright, which included honoring our elders. Being raised this way, I was obligated to care for him. It felt natural.

"When my mother began to decline, I cared for her, too. For two years I slept in her bed with her, because the dementia was so pronounced. I had to be there to help, to clean up after her. It was not easy. She was the sweetest person, but once the dementia set in, at times she became obstinate and angry. I was always concerned. Was she going to go out the gate into the street? Did she poop and pee on the floor again? Once she even threw her walker at a family member trying to care for her. Then she fell down. We had to take her to the ER. She told them the person was trying to shoot her. It was like living in a hell realm for everyone.

"The Dharma teachings on compassion were my armor, protecting me from erupting in frustration and shielding us all from anger. I also thought of how she cared for me so tenderly and patiently while raising me. I remember being a child falling asleep with my head on her lap as she cleaned my ears with a bamboo ear-cleaning stick. It was so calming. I felt so cared for. I wanted to give that to her, too. Being in touch with the circle of life was my liberation.

"Here I am nearing the end of my seventh decade, and I finally found a way to communicate in a consciously healing way with my *mizuko*, my water child.[1] I learned about the Japanese Buddhist mizuko ritual, which helps me acknowledge the loss and engage in an ongoing relationship by doing the simple acts of lighting a candle, offering incense and flowers from the garden, and a little treat. It gives me an embodied connection with my mizuko, enabling me to express respect both to my mizuko and myself. I do it quietly by myself on the twenty-fourth of the month. It is the auspicious day for Jizō Bodhisattva.[2] Jizō's compassionate focus is to usher beings through different realms, holding a special place for mizuko. Mizuko are beings who returned to primordial waters without setting foot on the earth and await auspicious conditions to return.

"In a way, caring for caterpillars in my garden and watching them change is a mizuko ritual for me. Not all of them make it. It happens before your eyes. It's watching life and death. It happens in a short period of time. It's a beautiful thing to watch the colors change, too, from yellows and greens to black pupa. It is a sublime wonder to watch the wings expand as they drip dry before taking flight. Observing this phenomenon is a meditation on metamorphosis.

"As I age, my friends age. More of them are facing infirmity, disease, and intense diagnoses. I, too, have had brushes with diagnoses and conditions that remind me that I am part of the circle of life and death."

After hours of conversation, Saya handed me a poem. It bubbled up in her heart after she was honored as an elder in her current sangha, which was a few weeks before we met. She says that poems sometime come to her, usually indicating a bud of new growth.

Buddha Was Asleep in Our Home[3]

Buddha was asleep in our home.
As a young child,
I never knew.
He didn't need to show himself in statues and icons.
He lived in the hearts of my people.
They embodied his way and shared his teaching.
He was happy. He could rest.

I found traces he was living with us . . .
Much later,
After much time had passed.
I was unaware . . .
I just thought they were
My grandmother's things.
I found the prayer beads.

I walked in a huge circle
To come home.
A long, winding circle
Called life.
I'm almost finished.

Today, I live with Buddha again.
I have a new home,
I found a new family that lives with Buddha.

Maybe I can live without the icons and images.
But now
It's a different time.
I'm lucky to live
Without the fear.
And, I like
All the images of the Buddha,
Especially the ones
That look like I belong too.

I found home.
I'm so happy.

Saya's poem reminds me of the women's poems in the *Therigatha*. Saya is finally free from the suffering she and her family endured due to racism, xenophobia, and her personal life choices. Open expressions of Dharma are now a source of comfort and strength, though her experience tells her that the most important expression of Dharma is that which animates her heart.

13

RECOVERY AND RESILIENCE

(TWENTY-FIRST CENTURY C.E., UNITED STATES)

Louise pauses as a tear seeps out. She had agreed to share her life experiences with me because Dharma has been transformative in her life. I saw a woman of confidence, clarity, and kindness. Until then, I had no idea about the depth or nature of the suffering that carved her heart out to be spacious enough to simultaneously hold despair, joy, and love. Her experiences, unfortunately, are not singular. Numerous people have faced conditions similar to what befell her family. Fortunately, with dedicated effort, Louise learned to wield Dharma to heal from the suffering.

"The death of my sister was the hardest thing I ever had to experience. I did have a teacher who was very kind. I did turn to the *Heart Sutra* as a serious, serious source of comfort. Just trying to understand no sickness, no old age, and no death. Walking around the whole of my life, everywhere, on the streets, driving my car, just trying to hold on to that raft and also let it penetrate me. I was sewing my *rakusu* (Buddha robe) in preparation for taking precepts (*jukai*), so with every stitch I was taking refuge.

"My teacher was unbelievably kind. His kindness was just a beautiful thing to help me get through that. Then going deeply,

deeply toe to toe with impermanence and ultimately coming to the realization that yes, this is heartbreaking, but there is fundamentally nothing wrong going on here. It's my idea that she's young. She shouldn't die. I love her. She shouldn't die. We survived a horrible childhood together. She shouldn't die. One by one, going through these very strong fixed ideas, excavating them, and exploring them. Then despite my own personal preferences really resting in . . . there's absolutely nothing wrong going on.

"I was nineteen years sober, and she was eighteen years sober when she died. She was married with two kids.

"I came to Buddhism two years after entering recovery. I was a motivated Catholic in my youth, but I awakened to the patriarchy there and the unanswered prayers. I became agnostic. Eventually something came online spiritually. Buddhism was in the background, and I wanted to explore it. I was afraid, however, to go into a big building, a big institution. A friend invited me to go in with her. I went through those doors like I went through the doors of recovery, and I have never stopped. I never left. I listened to Dharma cassettes. Dharma was in my head. When my sister, Emma, was diagnosed, Dharma went into my body. Dharma was my refuge.

"We grew up in an award-winning dysfunctional family. Emma was ten years younger than me. Another sister was seven years younger. My older brother and I were two years apart. My brother got the worst of it physically. When it would get very ugly, which was usually at night, I would take my younger sisters out of the house and take a walk to keep them out of the environment. If it was super late at night, I'd get them in my bedroom. I locked the door to give some sense of separation and protection, but the lock was weak. So, we'd sit with our backs to the door to keep our father out. Mother, too, would join us. Loud sounds, shouting, craziness, vulgarity, pounding on the bedroom door punctuated our life. My mother was a wonderful mother to me, more than good enough.

She was a fierce supporter. She was protective and nurturing. She encouraged me to soar.

"As adults, Emma and I would speak five to ten times a day. We exchanged joyful and frustrating moments in life. We celebrated good report cards by getting frozen yogurt or going to Six Flags. 'How is your day going?' 'I forgot to bring the lunches when I dropped the kids off at school.' We were each other's person.

"The floor fell out when she called to tell me about the breast cancer diagnosis. I remember everything about that moment, flip phone in hand. I was in my living room with walls of pinkish beige. The late afternoon sun was flooding in through a nearly floor-to-ceiling window. It streamed over a table with orchids that loved being in that spot, across a creamy white loveseat, illuminating patterns on the rug. I faced an old stone Buddha head on the mantel in the corner, the sun shining directly on it. I remember how the sun cast a shadow of the Buddha on the wall. A seated Buddha was on a Japanese *tansu* chest behind me. I thought, I am held. I am absolutely held by this. These are my two anchors that are going to hold me steady no matter what happens.

"Emma called the next day and said, 'I've thought about it and no matter what happens I am not going to drink or use any drugs.' In recovery we talk about going to any length to stay sober. That has been such a profound teaching for me that this young woman with two young kids said that to me at that time. That's the sincerity and depth of her practice. I totally resonated with this. As I sewed my rakusu, I committed to go to any length to stay in this practice of 'do no harm,' of doing no harm out of addiction. Twining Dharma and recovery, that's how we are going to get through this. Sewing vow, breath by breath. Taking refuge.

"Seventeen months of facing breast cancer began when she found a lump on her breast in the shower. Driven to know, she even went to the lab to get the results, not waiting for the doctor to contact her. Emma called me. On her deathbed, she asked me to watch over and care for her kids. They were six and eight. Emma and her husband had met in recovery and were committed to raising their children free from the suffering of an active addictive family. He traveled for work for months at a time. She knew I would help be a steady anchor for her children, and she trusted I would help them navigate life. It was spring. Emma did not live to see my jukai precept ceremony.

"Early on, parenting was about finding ways to hold them steady. Being with my girls, I gained an intuition about what Dogen as a child went through when he lost his father and then his mother. The depth of impermanence both Dogen and my girls felt is more than I can imagine. I so love Dogen for trying to understand this form of suffering and to transform it. Dogen was a model for how to approach impermanence and integrate grief. Dogen helped normalize my kids' experience. People lose parents. That was what I aimed to do with my girls, help them transform that suffering.

"With love and support from their father, grandma (our mom), and the mothers of the girls' friends, they never lacked for love. There was no interruption of love. They both did struggle, though. Grief showed up in decreased performance in school and sometimes was expressed through anger and defiance. They both had something. We reminded them that we would just keep loving them until they learned to love themselves. That's a lesson from recovery. We repeated their mother's motto: 'We love people for what's in their heart.' I introduced them to Buddhist teachings I thought would be helpful, such as loving-kindness, both for yourself and for those with whom you have difficulties. I aimed to model the Bodhisattva path of living compassionately.

"We often began meals together with the Buddhist chant:

> We reflect on the effort that brought us this food and
> consider how it comes to us.

> We reflect on our virtue and practice, and whether we are
> worthy of this offering. We regard it as essential to keep
> the mind free from excesses such as greed.
> We regard this food as good medicine to sustain our life.
> For the sake of enlightenment we now receive this food.
>
> First, this is for the Three Treasures;
> Next, for the four benefactors;
> Finally, for the beings in the six realms.
> May all be equally nourished.
> The first portion is to end all evil;
> The second is to cultivate every good;
> The third is to free all beings.
> May we all realize the Buddha Way.

"They are now upright, young adults. They carry the sacred wound. Cultivated through faith and love they fully embody their lives. They have grown up wise and compassionate beyond their years. I wish my sister was still here, but we weathered it. We got here, but at a high price."

Louise nurtured her family in ways that freed them from an intergenerational legacy of addiction and shepherded the next generation through traumatic loss. A foundation in Dharma fortified her with the strength to be compassionate during times of deep need.

14
TRANSMUTING BETRAYAL

(TWENTY-FIRST CENTURY C.E., UNITED STATES)

Though I did not know much about Tina when we first sat down to talk, she exuded the kind of warmth that often arises out of recovering from deep hurt. It turns out she, too, had misplaced the entrustment of her heart. The way she found out, however, was harshly dramatic and the consequences were severe. The suffering that is generated from realizing one had been deluded in a conjugal relationship often intensifies the poisons of both attachment and anger.

Bitterness and distrust can fester for years if conscious effort to heal is not pursued. Tina has spent the last handful of decades actively healing, and she is thriving now. Her willingness to share her story, nonetheless, requires courage and demonstrates her concern for others who might face similar situations. In her recounting of the events, she focuses on the aspects of the situation that she deems relevant for dissolving the negativity she experienced. It also brings into high relief that having access to women's stories reveals a treasure trove of wisdom for applying Dharma to intense real-life issues.

Tina and her husband of twenty years were asleep in the bungalow they called home. Their three teenagers were in their rooms. The ringing phone disrupted the quiet of their Berkeley abode. The answering machine speaker on their nightstand broadcast a strange female voice looking for Tina's husband. "I worry about you when I don't know where you are. Call me." Shocked silence reverberated through their bedroom, unleashing an avalanche of pain.

Tina's dream of family life ruptured in a nanosecond. How deep did the lies go? Was their love ever real? The disintegration of her marriage left her feeling worse than discarded garbage. She quickly needed to find a new place to live. The two oldest kids, daughters, were about to leave home anyway. The son had the hardest time. He had to change schools. He cried and cried. Tina can still hear him crying, "Is he going to love the other family more than us?" The father enticed their son to live with him, so he didn't have to pay child support.

For many years after the divorce, Tina dedicated herself to earning enough money to support herself. Early on, she had three jobs to make ends meet. Her family helped her rent her first place. It not only helped Tina in a concrete practical way, but it also tempered the erosion of her sense of lovability. But it was a tough stretch of years. She drew on strength buried deep in her bones. It took years to recover and carve out a new way of living. Tina had cordoned off her anger during the years of struggling to meet daily needs, but that did not abate the ire roiling inside her. After she had done much hard work, and all her children were adults, Tina eventually had the breathing room she needed to focus on tending to the wounds in her heart. She sought the wisdom of Buddhist teachings.

After reading several Dharma books, Tina decided to join a sangha near her home. At first while sitting silently, it was not quiet in Tina's mind. "Emotions and thoughts coursed through me," she said. "Like so many pebbles being thrown into a pond. The ripples collided with each other as they spread out across my mind. But I sat with them. Over time, the internal disturbances subsided. Like muddy water, when you let it be still, the sediment settles and clarity arises. Slowly, a calming quiet dawned. I noticed

I increasingly felt steady. I could see more clearly as the anger and negative emotions eased off. Not being continuously seized by the erosive poisons of indignation, resentment, and self-doubt, familiar delusions about life began to fade. I used to find comfort in those delusions that masqueraded as dreams.

"It's the loss of the dream that was hard, but I began to see that perfection is not what you live. Life is never going to be what you dreamed. Life is not that way. All the causes and conditions change. It's a moving target. Things deviate from the dream. When we lose something, our first instinct is to want to hold on and get it back. It can be an intoxicating delusion. This is life. How things are is not always what we want. I began to accept that life was not as I had thought it was.

"I resolved most of my anger through quiet sitting. Listening to Dharma teachers has also helped me make that shift. There's an art to talks delivered as teachings. Weekly teachings of kindness, humility, and compassion begin to change one's perspective on life. Over time, you get a sense of what something means, how to perceive things, and how to incorporate it into your life."

It took Tina years to reconfigure her perception of who she was. She plumbed the depths to disentangle the roots that had bound up her heart and that had convinced her that she was not worthy of love and became comfortable with trust again. She revised the narrative she had constructed about herself. Not only does she understand that she is lovable, but she has also learned to love herself more deeply. She is a friend who cares in concrete and profound ways, often appearing on ill friends' doorsteps with food. Sometimes she brings her toothbrush, too, so she can stay with them when they need assistance to get through the night. Her love flows from a deep well of understanding that is fed by the healing waters of Dharma, a spring infused with the wisdom of compassion.

15

RIDING WAVES OF GRIEF AND LOVE

(TWENTY-FIRST CENTURY C.E., UNITED STATES)

I was eager to talk with Megumi, a woman deeply committed to addressing communal suffering. She spends much of her time offering support to vulnerable populations. Whether she is volunteering with incarcerated people to support their "journey of meditation, healing, and transformation" (which she has done by teaching various things, including math and art, for over twenty years), helping a person navigate life outside of prison walls, or protesting against violence and injustice locally and abroad, she treats each person she encounters with dignity and care. I wanted to understand in what ways her personal path fuels her serious, long-standing, and continuing engagement with social justice issues. Her life tapestry is colored by many hues of suffering. Threads from the Pacific War, the sudden death of her father, the mental illness and suicide of her mother, alcoholism, divorce, and raising children on her own are woven together to make a life that could well be dark and dreary. Yet, Megumi is a warm and energetic person, quick to reach out a helping hand. Through deep conversations, I discovered how she braids Dharma wisdom, liberating practices, and supportive sangha into her life and transforms the suffering into luminous shades of compassion.

Megumi was raised in a family that wove back and forth across the Pacific Ocean before and after World War II. Both her parents were born in the United States to Japanese parents, both went to Japan when they were still children, and both came back to the United States as teens.

"My parents met in Chicago as young adults," Megumi tells me. "They spoke Japanese with each other and were totally in love. They had a very tight relationship. My dad was a really kind and wonderful person. He could talk to anybody, and people really liked him. He was very loving and kind. My mom was injured. There was some unresolved trauma that I came to see in many nisei [second generation] women. I never knew what the trauma was. She and her sisters, my aunts, could be very kind, but there was anger, a lot of anger. My dad was my closest friend and hero. My mom could not live without him. When I was twelve, he did not make it through surgery for an aortic valve replacement. He had rheumatic heart disease that had not been treated since childhood.

"It was difficult times for most Japanese Americans. Mental health issues were rife. My mom masked her depression when my father was there to support her. She committed suicide three months after he passed.

"For years I was convinced my mom's death was an accident. Social workers came and worked with me to help me see that my mom had committed suicide. To my knowledge, there was no note. So, either way, she had overdosed on pills."

Megumi lived with her aunts after her mom had passed. She witnessed the zombielike quality of one of her aunts when she returned home from electroshock therapy treatment. "It was jarring to see her like that," Megumi confesses. "My other two aunts tried to commit suicide and did not succeed. I had really bad role models of women in my family, which made me determined that I would never end up in that kind of situation, ever."

Being part of the larger Japanese American community, including being active in a Buddhist temple, Megumi found her way.

She received a good education, married, and had children. Then her family ruptured again. This time the break was precipitated by her husband's alcoholism, which negatively affected the children and got to a point where Megumi knew she had to leave. The tough divorce left her heart raw. She sought full custody of her two children. Although her husband didn't want the kids, out of spite he sued for custody and had his mother raise them. "I was lost. I got an ulcer. I had to crawl I was in so much pain," Megumi shares. "My kids were two and five at the time."

In the midst of this heart-wrenching situation, a friend suggested the Buddhist teachings of Thich Nhat Hanh. "I read his books, listened to tapes, and went on several retreats with him," she continues. "Thich Nhat Hanh saved my life. I felt like he was speaking to me, to my heart. I joined a local sangha as Thich Nhat Hanh suggested, but they did not have anything for kids. I wanted my children to have a Buddhist upbringing, so I decided to join a local Buddhist temple like the one I had grown up in. I felt welcome, even as a single parent."

The Jodo Shinshu temple gave Megumi and her children a community, which was vital for their well-being since most of her family lived far away. The temple members became like family. "I wanted my children to grow up in a Buddhist community and to know that the Buddha was there for them," she said.

Megumi loved seeing her children enthusiastically join the community in making the traditional Japanese *omochi* rice cakes to celebrate New Year's. Along with forty other kids, from elementary to high school, they were integral to the production of steaming over five hundred pounds of sweet rice to make dozens and dozens of rice cakes. After the rice was pounded, the kids dusted their hands with *katakuriko* (potato starch) to shape the hot and sticky rice into mounds. After placing them on the long tables, they fanned the rows and rows of cakes to cool them enough to place them in boxes for people to enjoy over the holidays.

Now adults, Megumi's sons reflect on how they can appreciate that—although it was not fun at the time—staying after to clean up helped them grow to be responsible people. They learned they didn't want to be the type of person who doesn't help others, underscoring they learned this independently from parental pressure.

Megumi's sons also joined the temple community for the major summer ritual of Obon. Obon is a time for ancestors to come back for a few days, a chance to remember deceased loved ones and feel the well of gratitude rise. It is a communal way to express respect and honor for those who paved the way for you. The highlight of the rite is celebratory with *taiko* drums thundering the beat for Obon dances. Her sons even went to rehearsals and enjoyed learning the dances.

In addition to learning to remember and honor the deceased through Obon, they also attended some funerals growing up, both Christian and Buddhist. Megumi was moved by them reflecting on how they were glad they were Buddhists. The funerals were emotional for them. They found the Buddhist funerals helped them understand the teachings on the dynamics of impermanence, interrelatedness, and transformation, that our connections transcend life and death. Such teachings helped them learn to grieve and honor the dead in an intimate and meaningful way.

Although she participates in ongoing activities in a Japanese Jodo Shinshu temple, Megumi still considers Thich Nhat Hanh her root teacher. "One of the things that really resonated with me about Thich Nhat Hanh," she shares, "is that he takes Buddhism out of temples and into streets. He told us stories of burying bodies in the Vietnam War. It tears your heart apart to hear. They embodied so much compassion when they went out and risked themselves to bury the bodies. That inspired me. Engaging with living Dharma really touched my heart.

"Until then, I saw things in black and white. Thich Nhat Hanh's poem 'Please Call Me by My True Names' penetrated my heart in a way none of the Buddhist rituals and practices I had been raised with ever did. The part that opened my heart to a whole world of profound love was this:

> I am the twelve-year-old girl,
> refugee on a small boat,
> who throws herself into the ocean
> after being raped by a sea pirate.
> And I am the pirate,
> my heart not yet capable
> of seeing and loving.[1]

"He can see the pirate in himself. He went through the anger and hate. What a beautiful way to illustrate living compassion. It is not black and white nor good and bad, like I had thought. All of us have this Buddha-nature in us, and it matters what seeds we water. That was a huge thing for me to learn and moved me profoundly. I want to be there for people.

"I want to speak out and support people so what happened to people of Japanese descent in the United States during World War II does not happen to others." Megumi has been there and supported countless people over the decades. She has become an exemplar of living compassion on the streets, in prisons, in Dharma classrooms, and in her approach to daily life. The groups she has sponsored, organized, and facilitated in a rehabilitation center include marginalized, cultural, and nonviolence-focused groups as well as a community of Buddhists. Megumi also teaches arts in a way that focuses on the power of artistic endeavors to heal individuals and communities. All of her activities emphasize healing and peace.

Megumi found love in the autumn of her life. Through her social justice activities, she met a warm and understanding man who is likewise a social justice activist. As their relationship becomes more serious, opportunities for growth and healing arise. Though both are committed Buddhists, they are from different cultures, races, and life experiences. Realizing how distinct their embedded assumptions about the nature of self are gives rise to different communication styles and expectations. They turn to Buddhist teachings and practices to guide them as they navigate the richly textured landscape of their relationship. Listening deeply to things that hurt when said or things that hurt when not said is critical. They are both dedicated to growing their love and learning from and about each other. The caring quality of their interactions is testimony to their mature approach to relating. It also indicates how central to and important living the Bodhisattva vows is to their lives.

Often in a deep relationship, wounds of the heart—some buried inside for decades—come to the surface, often emerging through indirect dynamics. With thoughtful reflection, it is possible to trace the pain back to its root source. This occurred with Megumi and her partner when they had to move to a long-distance relationship due to a shift in work locations. Megumi found each parting after a visit stirred intense emotions. She felt forsaken, even though her partner was comforting and reassuring. Megumi realized that when the emotional response is disproportionate to the situation, it is often a sign that an old wound is trying to be heard.

It became clear to her that it was the unhealed wounds caused by the sudden loss of her parents that were making her feel vulnerable sixty-some years after losing her mother to suicide within months of her beloved father's sudden death. Megumi is ready to face the unresolved anger, fear of abandonment, and grief. The key to healing from the love she deserved but did not receive growing up is to grieve the loss of it. In the nondual space that ritual generates, she can finally cry to her mother. She can tell her mother that she is angry with her for leaving when she was deeply needed. As a daughter in her early seventies, she can also see that her mother had been angry, too—angry that her beloved husband had suddenly died—and that she, too, had wanted to be loved. She also realized that her mother had been angry with herself for not being able to give her daughter the love she deserved.

In front of the Buddha on her simple home altar, Megumi lights a candle. The glow opens a crack in the darkness of her heart. Clouds of incense hold her tender heart in the most loving way. In this safe and sacred place there is no birth and death. Megumi meets her father and mother here and they cry together. She asks her father to help her because it is hard to say she loves her mother. Megumi knows he will support her. She aims to heal and experience that she is her mother and her mother is her, just as Thich Nhat Hanh taught her. The loss of love that had inflamed anger, insecurity, and doubt heals more each time she meets her mother and father at her altar.

Grieving her parents in this way thaws a shadow that had frozen more than sixty years of accumulated pain in her heart. Megumi gradually integrates the loss of her parents and the love she did not receive due to their early passing. She is slowly healing from the sense of not being lovable—especially in light of her partner's recent relocation. Megumi is learning to navigate love with the challenges of a long-distance relationship. She is committed to learning to trust that she is loved and now welcomes how it organically unfolds.

Walking meditation is her most reliable path to peace. "It gets me through," she affirms. It enables her to feel a heart-to-heart connection reverberating through her. Megumi pauses reflectively, "Thich Nhat Hanh is there for me every step of the way, even after he transitioned." Megumi was recently invited to become a Dharma teacher, a *Dharmacharya*, at Plum Village in France, an order founded by Thich Nhat Hanh during the Vietnam War, and she formally joined them. She is now supported by her Plum Village Dharma family, and their love is inscribed in her heart. Having returned to her loved ones and community in California, she continues walking toward peace, love, and justice in our world.

16

RITUALS FOR LIVING AND DYING

(TWENTY-FIRST CENTURY C.E., UNITED STATES)

Namiko greeted me with a smile. Her demeanor of clear-minded poise shone through. As I listened to her story, I was deeply moved by her resourcefulness in finding ways to meet personal and communal needs. Namiko grew up witnessing her grandmother's unfaltering acts of hospitality to help those in need. This is how she learned Dharma. It was animated by warm hands reaching out to meet the needs of the people around her. This attuned her to see the suffering on people's faces, especially the suffering of those in her own community. She also learned that navigating cross-cultural currents is part of being Japanese American.

Namiko lives with keen awareness of the legacy of suffering generated by the World War II incarceration of people of Japanese descent, including US citizens. The incarceration not only wounded the US constitutional republic, it wounded thousands and thousands of families. Despite the fact that Japanese Buddhist communities and individuals were intent on maintaining their caring hearts, suffering percolated behind their tidy screens of politeness. Namiko gathered resources to help with this, too. As she matured, she started seeing that in a profound way, all people are in her community. After a near-death experience, she expressed this vision in the way she designed her own funeral.

"I almost died," she shares. "I threw up one liter of blood and was hospitalized." Nine months after she was released from the hospital, Namiko admits to me that she is scared to die, especially since she wants to live for her children. Faced with a direct experience of her own mortality, Namiko sought support.

As a licensed social worker who has been at the helm of nonprofit organizations, she is comfortable advocating for her own needs and uses her skillset to contribute to her family's Buddhist community. Sometimes the concerns she offers are not welcome, in part due to gender dynamics in the community. Her clarity, confidence, and expertise often receive a cool reception from the male-dominated leadership. Though there are some in the community who have been kind to her, it was notable that in her time of need, no one in a leadership position from the Buddhist community reached out to her to provide spiritual support.

Namiko's grounding in Buddhist ways began at home. Her family lived with her paternal grandmother who frequently housed people while they found jobs or relocated during World War II after leaving the West Coast to avoid incarceration under Executive Order 9066.[1] Her father remembers how it was commonplace to come home from school and find the house full of people who were staying with them. Helping others was just a way of life.

Even thirty to forty years later, sometimes traveling long distances, many of these "guests" continued to bring them vegetables to express their gratitude for her grandmother's kindness in their time of need. Such gifts would first be offered to the *butsudan*, a home Buddhist altar. Placing gifts on the home altar and lighting incense before enjoying the gift is a natural thing to do, and her now adult children do it naturally, too. The altar Namiko grew up with is currently in another family member's home, so she and her husband got one for their family. It is located centrally in their home on a designated table between the living room and dining room.

Namiko's family also actively engages in activities at their local Buddhist temple. Sutras are chanted in Japanese, making her feel at home. In a sense, chanting is where she finds refuge. The sacred sounds resonating through her body make her feel grounded. This is how she draws on a greater power and fortifies her strength.

Before she entered school, the language spoken at home and temple was Japanese. In addition to learning English when she entered the local public school, she had to learn to navigate a new culture. With few people of color at school, Namiko became facile at switching between the culture and language at school and the culture and language at home and at the Buddhist temple. These circumstances attuned her to the microdynamics of social injustices. Seared into her memory is the look of despair on a schoolmate's face as she deboarded the school bus. She was a ten-year-old First Nations girl who was being forced into foster care.

Over time Namiko learned more about suffering that destroyed people's lives. Her awareness of injustice arose out of personal observations and choice of career path. She became sensitive to how cultural dynamics affect people's daily lives, shaping their views of themselves and others. When the dynamics, assumptions, and expectations of different cultures are involved—whether arising internally or during interactions with other people—confusion, frustration, and pain often emerge from a minefield of misunderstanding, unspoken fears, and doubt about one's own worth and the intentions of others.

"I have a lot of strong, defiant women in my family," she attests. These women include her maternal grandmother, who refused to marry the man arranged for her and instead eloped to marry the man she loved. Her paternal grandmother had eleven children, though two died in early childhood. Her paternal grandfather died young due to alcoholism, and her grandmother raised the six youngest children by herself.

Namiko's grandmother had come to the United States as a picture bride. She is one among countless women who persevered through extremely challenging circumstances. These women dug deep into their beings to be strong enough to care for others. Even if they did not leave much of a written record of their accomplishments and insights, the evidence that they gained wisdom about how to work with the nature of reality is evident in the depth of positive qualities with which a significantly high proportion of their children engage life and contribute to society.

Namiko's mother was born in the United States, so she had US citizenship. But when her mother was five, her family was deported to Japan because Namiko's grandparents didn't have papers to stay in the United States. Life in their small, homogenous village was challenging because they were ostracized due to their association with the United States. Namiko's mom even gave up her US citizenship to try to fit in. In the mid-1950s, she returned to the United States all by herself. She was still unmarried at thirty, which was late for Japanese women at the time. There she met her husband, Namiko's father, and began living with her strong and generous-hearted mother-in-law.

Because Namiko's mom wanted her children to be skilled in steering through the racial and cultural landmines that people of Japanese descent faced, she stressed that they learn to care for themselves and be independent. So after graduating with a master's degree, Namiko began working. She continued to work after having children, and today working enables her to connect with a broad range of people and commit to activities that support communal and personal growth, which in turn assists her to be not only a better mother but to cultivate a society that serves a broad range of human needs.

To live actively and concentrate intently is part of her identity. It was the way she was raised: Reach out a hand to help people in need. Being busy and working hard to support her family, community, and society is a form of "self-medication" from injustice. She chose this active path over sinking into an internal abyss of despair as she became increasingly aware of the current of systemic unfairness that coursed through society. Namiko knows in her bones, personally and professionally, the tensions and quandaries of navigating a complex cultural landscape, especially for women.

Based on Namiko's experience, the Japanese American cultural landscape generally values a woman who communicates in subtle and nonverbal ways—a woman who prioritizes being harmonious, patient, and supportive of men, especially those in leadership roles. In contrast, the more diverse, though largely Euro-American, cultural landscape in which she works professionally generally values someone who thinks independently, clearly articulates their ideas, and draws on their competencies to support the group. Namiko knows how to switch back and forth, but she sometimes consciously shares her understanding and knowledge with the motivation to help support the interests of the Japanese American community. Such cultural boundary crossing is not always welcome, especially if a woman does it. Namiko is not alone in finding these dynamics frustrating, even disrespectful. She wonders if that is why no one from temple leadership came to check in on her after her brush with death.

Reflecting on how the institutional organization of the Buddhist temple she's involved with was not structured to support her needs, she expressed concern for others. We discussed how the Buddhist community might develop a position, such as a spiritual care coordinator, that is explicitly charged with reaching out to people and address their more personal and spiritual needs. The Japanese American cultural climate is caring, but it also values harmony in a way that quietly makes it difficult to share situations that are emotionally fraught. A stigma is associated with having family challenges, so it is rare for people to talk about them. Shame closes people off from each other and themselves.

Now an elder of the Japanese American Buddhist community, Namiko envisions reviving Japanese rituals that mark significant moments in life as a culturally appropriate way for people to open up and share their personal concerns and challenges. They might make it culturally conducive for the community to reflect on the varying needs of people going through different phases of life. Namiko sees promise in several traditional Japanese rites, including Shichi-go-san, the rite for children aged seven, five, and three;[2] Seijinshiki, the coming-of-age ritual; the sixtieth birthday marking entry into elder status; and a calendar of "unlucky ages," which depend on the Chinese zodiac sign under which one is born.

Shichi-go-san, traditionally celebrated on November 11—the eleventh day of the eleventh month—can be a time to share the changing needs of children, especially in light of the increasing concerns about how to navigate internet and digital modalities of playing and learning. It can also be a time for parents to voice their concerns and challenges of parenting and explore creative ways to support each other. Conversations initiated during activities related to the ritual might open avenues to mutually support each other and consciously resist comparing and competing, which would only inflame pressure and stress for all involved.

The coming-of-age ritual, Seijinshiki, might be another milestone to acknowledge as a community. Traditionally celebrated on January 15 in Japan, the ritual for becoming an adult is celebrated the year a person turns twenty, the age of majority in Japan. Since the age of majority is eighteen in the United States, modifying the age when the ritual is celebrated is warranted. Also, the challenges of going through puberty and becoming an adult are significantly more stressful now, so instead of having just a one-day event, a community could prepare and support youth with internal and external resources over the course of a year by offering curricula, retreats, and forums to face challenges together and receive guidance from skilled facilitators. It would be important to include space and time to process fears, pressures, and anxiety, so the activity does not become yet another venue in which one is expected to excel and appear perfect. The celebration at the end of the year would then be a meaningful rite of passage.

Turning sixty is a major traditional milestone that is celebrated by wearing a red garment on one's sixtieth birthday. It indicates that one is beginning the return to primordial waters from which people are born. The social significance of this ritual is to remind the community that the person may not be as strong or fast as before and that they may need to adjust their expectations of the person and be understanding, patient, and caring. With longevity being greater than it was when the tradition began, adjusting the age is likely warranted, perhaps to seventy-five or eighty. For the person celebrating their birthday, it is a chance to recognize that they are not alone in going through this passage, which might help them to accept the changes with more grace. Respect for elders is implicit in this ritual. So the person celebrated is socially elevated to the respected status of elder, a person to whom one turns to for experience-based guidance and knowledge.

Some Japanese traditions are related to the Chinese zodiac birth year. For instance, there is a calendar of *yakudoshi*, or "unlucky ages," in which troubles are more likely to occur, such as age 42 for men and age 33 for women. Casting them as "unlucky" years is a way to direct attention to the myriad of causes and conditions beyond individual control. There is a whole table of ages and birth years, ranging from 1-year-olds to 109-year-olds born in the Year of the Wild Boar and 10-year-olds to 118-year-olds born in the Year of the Tiger. In other words, in any given community, there will be people having a year in which hardships may flare up.

Having an ongoing ritual framework might encourage a community to acknowledge that everyone has years that are tough and help normalize people reaching out for help rather than hiding in shame. Ritualizing these phases of life indicates that no one is alone, making it easier to generate a safe space to be vulnerable and create connections that draw on the insights and strengths of the whole. Augmenting the celebratory dimensions of these rituals with reflective dimensions involves humility and courage yet in so doing the community is deepened and individuals receive needed support.

Thinking of such ways to meet the needs of others helps Namiko diminish her own suffering. Her current condition is such that she lives with the possibility that she could be "pushed off the cliff again." Brain fog related to her condition compromises her ability to be as active and focused as she had been. She is aware that she is also depressed, so she has reached out to First Nations friends who have given her the spiritual support she needs.

Exhibiting profound creative strength as she faces her own mortality, Namiko has prepared the details of her own funeral. Her spiritual maturity and freedom are evident in the way she weaves together elements from various traditions and people. A traditional Buddhist funerary ritual forms the framework of her interfaith funeral. She wants a song composed by young Japanese American Buddhists to be performed. She also wants a Methodist pastor friend to speak at her funeral.

Growing up around Indigenous people, she has always felt a sense of being kindred spirits. One of her close friends, a firekeeper, explained that each step of a dance on the earth heals the world. Moved by this, Namiko wants indigenous dancers and drumming to be included either during or after the indoor service. Namiko also knows a rabbi who said he would pray for her, and who asked his Jewish community to pray for her, too. She would like him to be a part of her funeral, as well.

Being treated with such warm concern touched her heart deeply in a world where not all people keep their word. She wants her Indigenous friends and the rabbi included in her funeral because they are the ones who came to her and provided the spiritual support she needed after her brush with death. She also wants to somehow weave in a Muslim friend and perhaps some bikers she worked with as part of her social work. They made it clear that they would protect her.

Namiko's interfaith funeral design integrates the rich spiritual sources that support her. The act of preparing her funeral expresses her confidence and affirms her view of Dharma: Respect and be grateful for others and support people in need, regardless of their spiritual tradition and cultural background. She designed her funeral to be a response to injustices done to people who are treated as "other." Her funeral will reflect her vision of a just world where all people are respectfully included, lovingly embraced, and integral to the interdependent nature of Dharma. With her big heart that values and cares for others, Namiko wields her liberating power in a diverse world.

REFLECTIONS

Dharma of Storytelling: Befriending Lotus Blossoms

Stories have fueled Dharma for over twenty-five hundred years. They have been adapted in each era, in each place, and in each community to inspire people to apply Dharma in their lives. Though women have been integral to this phenomenon, many stories about their activities have yet to be discovered and told, and others may never be known. We can amplify women's contributions by trumpeting the fact that without women nurturing enough people with Dharma activities to keep Dharma alive, the Buddhist tradition would not have lasted through the millennia and become the global network of wisdom teachings and transformative practices that guide and support those facing injustice, fear, difficult childbirth, crippling chronic pain, degenerative disease, and loss of loved ones. The stories in this book about women in particular communities at specific times gives a glimpse of the richly textured ways that women's hands, hearts, and minds have shaped the Buddhist tradition over the centuries.

Writing these stories introduced me to a cast of creative, resilient, and wise women. Whether historical, living, or plausibly imagined, they inspired and guided me. They taught me that the crowning act of wielding liberating power is to embody compassion in the various seasons and circumstances of life.

Mahaprajapati models this in raising Siddhartha as her own. Mali demonstrates in concrete and practical ways how to weave compassion into her busy daily life by waking up early to cook and feed monks, her children, and her ill sister. The seventh-century nun Lianlu recognizes that nuns unilaterally bowing to monks could feed the delusion of a separate and superior self. Her awareness illuminates the lesson that concern for even those who are taught to see you as inferior facilitates dissolving your own delusions and opens your heart to care. Facing the loss of her mother, Ayamé expresses her love by embroidering their hair together into an image of Kannon, with each stitch accepting the reality of impermanence and transforming their relationship. Kané epitomizes the kind of care older women often offer to young women as they go through the joys and fears of childbirth. She offers practical assistance along with spiritual guidance. After Obāchan lost her husband and son to war, she teaches us how releasing oneself from the grip of hatred frees space for warmth and peace. Saya and Megumi exemplify how grieving is a part of self-compassion. In the autumn of their lives, they process healing from the wrenching loss of loved ones early in life: one to abortion, one to suicide.

Collectively these women illustrate how once your compassion is no longer captive to the poisons of delusion, attachment, and hate, you are free to pour compassion on all in your midst, including yourself. Compassion changes how you perceive what is happening, enabling you to see how those who generate conditions of oppression are themselves suffering. The women herein manifest how wielding liberating power involves creatively unleashing compassion and courageously brandishing a sword of wisdom to cut off the causes of suffering.

All of these women became my *kalyāṇamitra*, my Dharma friends. In Sanskrit, *kalyāṇa* means "benevolent, virtuous, and generous." *Mitra* means "friend" or "the one who has been with us." May the women you met through these stories become your Dharma friends, too, for with the wise and compassionate ministrations of Dharma friends, we can blossom.

An exchange recounted in the Pali canon comes to mind:

> Ananda asks the Buddha, "Is it true that *kalyāṇamitra* are an important part of the spiritual path?"
>
> Buddha responds, "No, it is not true that *kalyāṇamitra* are an important part of the spiritual path. *Kalyāṇamitra* are the entirety of the path."

Dharma friends are integral to the Dharma path because they share the aim to dissolve delusion, attachment, and aversion. They are committed to being there and encouraging you along the path of enlightenment. Companions that call you to live in accord with your highest principles, they respect you and care about your well-being. Dharma friends listen to your heart and attune to your concerns, values, fears, and aims. They redirect you when you wander down an unhelpful path and uplift you when you are down. Dharma friends support us, make insightful observations, and walk with us.

Dharma friends are those who blossom in the mud and help us blossom there, too. They empower us by generating sympathetic resonance, much like the Chinese Buddhist concept of *ganying*. *Gan* is a stimulus and *ying* is a compassionate response. For example, a stimulus might be that one friend expresses anger over a recent event, and the other friend responds by observing the anger might arise out of shame over an unresolved issue stemming from the past. It takes astute insight to help effectively in such a situation. Since myriads of causes and conditions give rise to events, the skill required to meet suffering is often subtle, nuanced, and dynamic. In attuning to you and the fullness of the present moment, Dharma friends can set in motion waves of wise and compassionate energy. In other words, they see both the ways we suffer and our potential to be liberated. A Dharma friend, by definition, is a friend who does this.

Seeing the world through the eyes of a Dharma friend enables us to see both suffering and liberative healing. Doing so means becoming a Dharma friend to oneself. We are each our own oldest friend. We have been there through everything. We know intricate details about events, even things stored in our bodies that have faded from our conscious memories. To heal requires self-compassion—to see ourselves with a piercingly clear mirror that also reflects the vast web of interrelationships that support, protect, and generate us. To perceive this involves accepting ourselves in all our particularity, complete with the shame that blankets our hearts, the fear that quivers in our bones, and the delusions that muddle our minds. It also involves engaging with the forces that flow through the structures that organize specific sociohistorical contexts as well as the larger environmental conditions.

Being a Dharma friend to the world makes palpable the impact of narrow-minded, patriarchal, and small-hearted actions. Such exploits are potent and persistent. They produce layer upon layer of delusion that often diminish our sense of possibility and generate perceived obstacles to our liberation. They often distract us from our capacity to be compassionate. Approaching such situations in a relational, personal, emotional, and embodied way is to be a Dharma friend to the world. Doing so facilitates the flow of liberation in the world.

The key lies in flexibility and intimate responsiveness, like water moving through rocks in a river, caressing each stone—no resistance, only acceptance. The water does not experience a rock as being in its way or being in the wrong place. Water and rocks dance harmoniously. Rocks are the stimulus, *gan*, and the water is the compassionate response, *ying*. Over time the sympathetic resonance of rock and water transforms the landscape. Monumental changes occur as water offers its streaming ministrations to the rocks. The more we respond to the cries of the world as water responds to rocks, the better a Dharma friend we are to the world.

Indeed, water is a vital Dharma friend, providing the planet and all its beings with life-sustaining nourishment. Oceans, too, are among our most fundamental Dharma friends. Often described as the womb of our planet, oceans provide conditions to produce life forms and protect them as they take shape. Women's wombs, too, are Dharma friends. A woman's body generates the conditions for a life to grow, even funneling calcium from the mother's teeth and bones if needed to provide for the being growing inside her and channeling the interstellar heat that gave rise to iron that pumps through her heart so she can nurture the baby's heart.

Perceiving ourselves as Dharma friends activates our senses to attune to the whimpers in our midst. In response to the incalculable ways people harm, hold each other back, and worse, we can choose to be unflinching in our resolve to be compassionate, to alleviate suffering. We can write Dharma stories that invoke delusional practices to cultivate awareness of our interdependence, to model transforming hatred into clear peace. Being a Dharma friend enriches the quality of Dharma stories we can write because such stories immerse us in suffering and illuminate healing.

The Dharma friendships that grew out of relating to the women in this book—historical, contemporary, and imagined—were nourished by nine principles I developed to see women's strategies of wielding liberating power. The principles helped me see how women could and did liberate Dharma from the narrow lenses and oppressive forces of patriarchy and misogyny. They also helped me appreciate the ways women applied their liberating wisdom to a host of personal circumstances of suffering. Here are the nine principles I followed to interpret and write the Dharma stories in this book:

1. Sincerely care for suffering to stop.
2. Make space for not knowing.

3. Look through expansive and contextualized lenses.
4. Account for our interdependence.
5. Navigate with one eye on ideal aims and another eye on raw realities.
6. Move through an embodied perspective.
7. Assess whether a teaching or practice generates suffering.
8. Assume women want to stop suffering.
9. Envision past women full of power facing adversity.

Each principle is described in detail in the sections below.

1. SINCERELY CARE FOR SUFFERING TO STOP

To sincerely care is a powerful force. It drives awareness, focuses concentration, fuels creativity, and energizes action. To sincerely care protects against indifference, callousness, and despair. It helps the heart and mind be flexible, strong, and warm, undergirding persistence. When you sincerely care, you are compelled to find a way to help. You do not wait for better conditions to arise. You envision a path beyond suffering. You galvanize your creativity to seek effective responses with what is available. It surges when possibilities are detected.

Writing and perceiving stories about wielding liberating power, however, is a humbling and daunting undertaking. It requires honesty, integrity, and healing. We must summon our courage to face how our world is saturated with horrific injustices and how we are affected by them and/or contribute to them. The inertia of sociopolitical economics that were deliberately engineered to depend on people's suffering dominates the institutionalized halls of power. People designed systems to establish themselves at the expense of others and set into motion a torrent of suffering. We cannot control how others behave, yet we do influence the conditions in which we act.

Seeing and writing a Dharma story opens us up to awareness of how we perceive and treat ourselves, to become attuned to the varying degrees of harmful and helpful. Anger, self-loathing, and depression are common responses to suffering. Be a Dharma friend to yourself. Sincerely care enough to stop generating suffering in yourself. Forgive yourself for feeling you are not good enough, strong enough, smart enough, pretty enough, or any such judgments that interfere with your capacity to care. This is a vital act of compassion. Generating conditions that support yourself can lead to realizing everyone is worthy of compassion. In this way, your suffering can be a portal to connect with others who likewise suffer. Such connections wrought in vulnerability and pain can open pathways of liberating power.

To sincerely care for yourself and others, to stop suffering is key to reading or writing a Dharma story.

2. MAKE SPACE FOR NOT KNOWING

In pouring a cup beyond overflowing, a Zen tea master schooled an overconfident student that you cannot learn anything new if you do not begin with an empty cup. Likewise, it is beneficial to remind ourselves how little evidence is available to know how most people thought and felt throughout history, especially those without resources or inclination to record their own contributions. It behooves us to also keep in mind that the lack of evidence is not evidence of lack. Not knowing is to be open, to be courageous enough to stay porous, to be vulnerable.

Drawing on the "fabric of reality" metaphor, I see my project of exploring women's Buddhist activities as loosening up the weave of the dominant narrative that is largely woven with threads men chose to include. By creating space in the fabric of reality for women's vast and complex contributions to history and Buddhist culture, we acknowledge that there is much we do not know. Unless we know details about how women spent their days and what they thought and felt, we cannot conclude they were insignificant. In consciously foregrounding the countless neglected threads from our current version of the fabric of reality, we allow for new information, insights, and perspectives. We open up space to explore, imagine, and breathe.

Reading between the lines can loosen the weave of the narrative fabric. Some words can be windows through which to see through the words that insidiously hide women's power. Other words might obscure the fuller dynamics of the context in question. These words include *official*, *acknowledged*, *recognized*, *authority*, *institution*, *permission*, *allow*, *rule*, *practice*, *tradition*, and *misogyny*. With each of these words, examine from whose perspective the statement is made. For example, ask, "Recognized by whom?" "Whose authority? Do all relevant parties accept that authority?"

Question if the statement assumes that all people have agency. If it does not, then it is an incomplete narrative that furthers the agenda of those who are considered to have agency. Might there be other groups that disagree, resist, or have their own ways? If so, the scope of the claims is limited and does not reflect the full picture. *Misogyny* is a word that can be used to point out unfairness, but it can also be used in ways that obfuscate women's agency, creativity, and contributions. People are affected by misogyny, but they are not defined by it. There is always a response. Note special metaphors for diminishing or dismissing the contributions of women. Women are often depicted as being on the "margins," but they are also often in the center of the home and temple life where future members of society are being raised and shaped. These principles aim to elucidate such responses. I encourage you to sleuth for more, for this is not an exhaustive list.

Making space for not knowing promotes identifying what we do and do not know, enables us to base our analysis of a situation with an open mind, and encourages us to creatively explore and imagine strategies of liberation that the dominant narrative has not highlighted.

3. LOOK THROUGH EXPANSIVE AND CONTEXTUALIZED LENSES

Given the sleuthing nature of recovering or imagining how women might wield liberating power, it is beneficial to look through both expansive and contextualized lenses. An expansive view facilitates situating matters in larger cross-cultural streams over centuries, which elucidates ongoing continuities and changes. Looking through a contextualized lens brings to the fore specifics of particular sociohistorical, cultural, linguistic, and local dynamics. Together, these foci of exploration bring into view the complex causes and conditions that give rise to developments. To see any specific event in the context of its broader surroundings is critical to ascertaining the impulses coursing through what has occurred or is transpiring.

Oscillating between wide-ranging and tightly focused perspectives can generate insights that arise from juxtaposing shifting viewpoints. Decentering and recentering information promotes fresh awareness, often bringing to light concerns, concepts, and values that influence people. In the process, aspects of the tradition that have not been woven into the predominant narrative can surface. Once we glimpse more pieces of the fabric of reality, we can pull on the threads and weave them into our open-ended narrative.

4. ACCOUNT FOR OUR INTERDEPENDENCE

Assuming a deep and broad frame of reference facilitates recovering or imagining women's contributions to the Buddhist tradition. Since we depend on a myriad of relationships, being inclusive captures a fuller swath of the reality in which things unfold. Accounting for our interdependence illuminates the fact that nothing occurs in isolation, and everything has ramifications. It beckons us to not ignore, dismiss, or discount anyone in our effort to understand ourselves.

The Buddhist teachings excel at explanations of the self. The earliest echelons of the tradition purport that the nature of self is *anatman*, or no-self. That is, self is not a separate independent entity. It is an ever-changing aggregate of activities that are easy to perceive as an enduring and discrete thing. That it is an impermanent construct is central to how liberation from suffering is possible. Realizing that there is no fixed and separate self, our interdependence becomes palpable. We begin to notice our connections, which in turn affects our actions. When we move with consciousness of our interdependence, we awaken to how it enables both oppression and liberation. Our interdependence is a dance of fluid relationships. Oppression occurs when we act out of delusion, desire, and hatred. Liberation occurs when we clearly and creatively face the moment without grasping or rejecting.

The crux of interdependence is a koan: How do we wield liberating power in a context that is replete with oppressive institutions, teachings, and practices?

5. NAVIGATE WITH ONE EYE ON IDEAL AIMS AND ANOTHER EYE ON RAW REALITIES

As with any effort to fathom human activity, it is crucial to explore what people face in their lives, aspire to, and assume about reality. Not losing sight of ideal aims safeguards against the imagination-dulling effects of bitterness and cynicism. It minimizes missing or undermining people's potential, especially those challenged with unjust treatment. Keeping an eye on raw realities safeguards against ignoring, diminishing, or dismissing the experiences of people, especially those who are perceived to be inferior. Just as a lifeguard keeps their attention on the person they are swimming out to save, maintain focus on the purpose of your effort. Whether it's working on a scholarly project for career advancement or empowering people to ameliorate suffering, this approach can yield critically sophisticated scholarship and inspire creative ways to respond to suffering. These are not necessarily contradictory motivations.

By keeping in sight the ideal vision of the cessation of suffering and the actual conditions of suffering, we can respond effectively, even in harsh conditions. The remedy is to see through eyes of compassion.

6. MOVE THROUGH AN EMBODIED PERSPECTIVE

Bodies are not generic. They are concrete and specific. No two are the same. Each one is a construction of a host of elements and influences. The main elements include body features (size, genitalia, sense organs) and colors (skin, hair, eyes). The main influences include the historical epoch in which one lives, culture, sociopolitical economics, personal experience, language, familial relations, education/skill, and gender identification.

Realizing the complexity of working with bodies is critical to employing an embodied perspective. Recognizing the full and fluid spectrum of body designations, including female, male, nonbinary, and transgender, is fundamental. I am aware that my use of the term *woman* flies fast and loose with reality and is in tension with the very embodied perspective I advocate. Therefore, I encourage you to transpose the term as is suitable to your concerns and be patient with the imprecise and incomplete nature of anything I say about "women." Also keep in mind that a statement about women does not necessarily imply something exclusive to women or negative about nonwomen. I actively resist invoking the Buddhist concept of emptiness here because it is often used to dismiss the harsh reality of marginalized people. When concerned with alleviating suffering, it's expedient to remember emptiness is form.

How do you see from an embodied perspective? You see signs of fertility in nature, affirming a woman's sense that she naturally belongs. What comes into focus when you take bodies with wombs seriously? You see they are powerful creators, indispensable for the survival of the species. What do women hear? Cries of their babies, giggles of delight, shrieks of surprise, students asking questions. What do women smell? Garlic sautéing, food burning, soiled diapers, flowers, incense. What do women touch? Bloody wounds, feverish foreheads, soft cheeks, ripe fruit, dirty clothes, computer keyboards, hot pans. What do women taste? Soup, salty sweat, bitter medicine. What do women think? When will the fever break? What is there to make for dinner? What is the best word to express my idea? What does my child need? How do I comfort my dying mother? Today is precious.

An embodied perspective of Buddhist liberation is practical. It is not a veiled attempt to essentialize people. It examines whether a teaching mitigates suffering. It experiments with a practice to ascertain if it meets a need. If not, then one explores other routes until an effective one is found. An embodied perspective does not tarry on abstract notions of right/wrong or good/bad for it sees morality and virtue as acts that do not cause suffering. It seeks ways to cultivate loving-kindness and compassion. It promotes identifying and analyzing the dynamics of a situation as well as prompt potential liberating strategies.

7. ASSESS WHETHER A TEACHING OR PRACTICE GENERATES SUFFERING

The Buddhist tradition is replete with guidance on how to navigate compassionately through the mires of suffering. Unfortunately, there are instances where such offerings are the source of, rather than the antidote to, suffering. Dharma teachings and practices are those that after having been tested are verified to effectively liberate beings from suffering. What is helpful for some, however, might not be helpful for others. Moreover, absence of conscious intention to cause suffering does not mean that suffering does not result. Our interrelatedness notwithstanding, teachings and practices that may be skillful in one situation may not be in another.

Though the Buddhist tradition offers guidelines, each being must experiment with what is conducive to their situation. Hence, the proliferation of sutras and practices continues. Teachings and practices that cause suffering arise out of matrices of communal and personal suffering. It is important to discern the difference, for teachings and practices that cause suffering have been incorporated under the vast umbrella of the term *Buddhism*. Ascertaining that which effectively allays suffering is the key to wielding liberating power.

Analysis is required to discern whether a historical or contemporary practice, rule, or teaching might help reduce suffering. If there is evidence of ignorance, greed, or aversion, it is likely to cause suffering. Ask: Does it exhibit ignorance of impermanence, interdependence, and nondual wisdom? Does it promote divisiveness, inflame anger, or incite hatred? Does it lure one into short-term gain, materialism, or selfish aspirations? Noting whether something is motivated by the poisons will assist us in dissolving the delusion upon which structural, institutional, textual, and personal oppression is based. It is especially important to do so if the rhetoric supporting systematic suffering draws on teachings found in a sutra—the purported word of the Buddha—or practices upheld by people in the highest echelons of institutional power.

It behooves us, therefore, to be vigilant in assessing whether teachings or practices have the potential to be oppressive. Notice whether the people who advocate the teachings or practices hold positions of structural power. Consider the substantiation offered to support a pronouncement, especially if it asserts inferiority or incapacity of some people. If no proof is offered or the reasoning is not compelling, resist accepting the assertion, even if it is in a text ascribed as scripture or authoritative and if it is made by a person broadly recognized as a leader or teacher. The same is true for scholarly interpretations of those teachings and practices.

In the process of identifying that which is effective, it is important to humanize authors of sutras and teachers of practices. When encountering a situation that produces suffering, blaming, shaming, or accusing are understandable responses. In being inherently divisive and driven by incomplete perspectives, however, they do not extract the root of a problem. Nonetheless, understanding the dynamics behind actions that cause suffering is central to sorting out what ameliorates suffering. It involves measured reflection and is not quick to generalize or judge. It is not a veiled way to find excuses for perpetrators and blame victims, nor does it exonerate discrimination. Sometimes the compassionate response to teachings and practices is not to follow them, for they are not effective in helping you stop suffering.

8. ASSUME WOMEN WANT TO STOP SUFFERING

To assume women (really, everyone) want to stop suffering is humanizing. It acknowledges sentience and highlights self-respect and agency. Anticipating a person's motivational drive, it facilitates discerning what they might have cared about and what they thought was worth working hard for. Imagine women experimenting with ways to ease the hardships that often attend birthing, nourishing, clothing, and housing a family, nursing the sick, and caring for the elderly and dying. Except for birthing, these activities are not necessarily "women's work." They are essential work, though, and women tend to perform this work. To acknowledge that such work is often done by women is not to relegate them to such work. Rather, it validates the women who make these critical contributions to their community. Reflecting on what would not be possible without this work is a way to see what women valued and deemed worthy of their support.

Recognizing women's activities as integral to the functioning of communities will yield a more dynamic understanding of the challenges people face. To balance the abundance of information about what men thought and did, intentional effort is required to recover and understand women's contributions. Keeping in focus the needs, resources, and challenges of the whole community will enable us to discover important endeavors that were accomplished by women. It is important to not isolate women's work, for doing so might lead to the same types of distorted and limited narratives that were generated by looking just from a man's perspective at what men did.

Leaning in and listening to the types of suffering women encountered will help us appreciate their ingenuity, resilience, and wisdom. No one makes it through birthing and child-rearing without facing fears and frustrations. No one makes it through life without getting sick and hoping for relief. Everyone meets death, often stirring introspection. Women are often the ones in the room to whisper words of encouragement or offer an understanding look. In the midst of these activities, many women were subject to men's delimiting views of women, intensifying the obstacles women navigated. That so many people survived childhood and many even make it into old age indicates that women developed ways to allay suffering and cultivate life-sustaining wisdom.

9. ENVISION PAST WOMEN FULL OF POWER FACING ADVERSITY

Through stories, imagine how women wielded liberating power in response to negative treatment, structures, or environments in the past. The historical evidence of what women did and thought conveys a promising picture. The historical women mentioned in this book are inspiring examples. Two imperial women exercised their power to enact their vision of a world where women received support and guidance in their efforts to ease suffering. Mahaprajapati in India responded to the need to care for her sister's child and raised him as a son who grew into a compassionate and wise leader. She herself then led women along the path of wisdom and compassion. Empress Kōmyō in Japan founded a nunnery that continues training women in transformative study and practice of the Buddhist teachings, which enables them to serve those who come through their gates. They carry on the legacy of Empress Kōmyō, who bathed an extremely filthy person with her own hands, overcoming her initial hesitation by the force of her vow to care for others.

Even though most of women's activities are shrouded by historical distance or obscured by androcentric values, what we can glean from the information we have indicates women navigated the complex terrain of sociocultural expectations, life challenges, and aspiration to cease suffering with a host of skills, concerns, and courage. Highlighting how some women wielded liberating power offers a glimpse of what was possible and inspiration for what is probable. To understand or speculate about how women wield liberating power, we need to both acknowledge the obstacles and discern what would effectively stop the suffering. Doing so involves assessing what kind of actions and thoughts are skillful. It involves attending to how actions and thoughts can effectively be tailored for specific situations.

Focusing on sense experience with awareness of our intimate interdependence can help one discern how to move compassionately in response to a particular need. For example, our senses enable us to hear a person crying out of grief, cuing us to offer the compassionate response of sitting quietly in their presence. Respecting their loss fosters connections to those who have passed on, engendering a sublime experience of the nature of interdependence, that death is radical change, not total separation. Such tender presence is a potent way to wield liberation, such as how Kakushinni cared for her father, Shinran, as he aged and passed on, or how Louise cared for her sister's daughters after her sister passed. None of these activities betray a hint of being compromised because they were done by and for females.

Other situations might require one to summon fierce determination, such as Empress Wu defying the sutras that asserted a woman could not be a chakravartin and establishing the Zhou dynasty to rule the country like a mother; Abbess Jizen moving against the erosive force of centuries of neglect—stemming from financial support being withdrawn from nuns' temples and not monks' temples—and restoring rigor and elegance to Hokkeji; Louise leaning against a bedroom door to protect family members from a raging alcoholic father; and others who did not surrender their hearts to the deleterious forces of racism, infidelity, and misogyny.

Self-care can be an act of liberation, as in the case of Saya, who engaged in rituals to heal from an abortion fifty years earlier, or Namiko, who designed her own funeral to be inclusive, healing herself from the pain of having a near-death experience that elicited no response from a male minister. Numerous women care for others as their way of wielding liberating power, as did Eshinni who cared for herself and others through an epidemic and famine, never intimating she was limited in life or in death because she was female. Though nameless, countless mothers throughout history who lost sons to war found a way to resolve hate and continue to care for the living.

Historically, a few women, including Empress Xu, manifested their liberative wisdom by joining the rarefied number of people who received a sutra. The sutra she received in a dream includes solid Mahayana teachings but is mostly composed of dharanis that people could chant in their times of need. Women also demonstrated their wisdom through liberative interpretations of Buddhist sutras, such as the thousands of nameless women who organized and lead Nineteenth Night groups. These women supported each other, especially regarding the challenges of giving birth, and interpreted the *Blood Pond Sutra* in a female-affirming way. Chan Master Jizong expressed her wisdom through poetry and recorded sermons that continue to guide and inspire women in transformative effort and insight.

Learning historical stories of women's contributions to the Buddhist tradition can inspire women today to create their own examples of women liberating Dharma for those in the future. We can tell ourselves our own stories in a way that helps us view our journeys in a dignified way. We can frame our experiences in a narrative of how we overcame challenges and responded with Dharma. Seeing our own lives as continuous with the lives of Buddhist women stretching across the millennia and around the globe places things in an ennobling context and can help us recognize the ways we are wielding Dharma in our everyday lives.

These Dharma stories are stimulating tales of acclamation. They erupt out of a primal instinct to interrupt efforts to render women invisible. They reveal ways women defy the perception that they are inferior and polluted. They lay bare the absurdity that women are incapable and insignificant. Moving against such headwinds, Buddhist women exude profound strength, wisdom, and compassion. May such Dharma stories inspire creative ways to relieve suffering.

Collectively these nine principles promote identifying and analyzing the dynamics of a situation, as well as prompt potential liberating strategies. These principles and stories do not disprove the evidence of suffering wrought by Buddhist teachings codified in sutras, practices, and institutional structures. Indeed, to be effective, the ways women have suffered within the context of the Buddhist tradition must be addressed. My aim is to offer guidelines to see through and beyond constricting and unedifying lenses of teachings and practices, to discern where Buddhist tradition is not in accord with the liberating wisdom of Dharma. By extending the sweep of our attention, we can expand our knowledge and understanding of women's ingenuity, insights, and strengths.

I invite you, too, to create a Dharma story about a matter that moves your heart and engages your concerns. It might revolve around a real or imagined person. It could focus on you or a loved one. It could center on a figure from sociohistorical events that shaped you or your community. It could be a chance to resolve issues that were painful.

You might enjoy imagining yourself as a recluse in a cave. Perhaps write a poem as if it were written by someone you respect. You could tell the tale of a female Buddhist figure you would like to be your teacher. It might be fun to add to the story about what Shakyamuni learned from women. Animate the ways an unknown woman generated beauty out of daily tasks and unknowingly sparked deep motivation in a person who went on to become a wise Dharma teacher. Compose a story about a ritual devoted to a particular woman or community and include eight different offerings (think of colors, smells, sounds) and say what they represent or mean.

You can add historical or fictive names to the list of women who have contributed to the Buddhist tradition, expressing respect and gratitude. Since myriads of potential teachers are missing from the record, you can augment possibilities by writing Dharma stories that serve as models for a range of situations or contexts women navigate. May your stories spur you, your friends, and future generations to seek ways to wield liberating power.

Seeking and discovering Buddhist women's liberating power and honing our imaginations to bring to life the Buddhist historical record and philosophical teachings, we can illuminate how women could—and have—tailored the Buddhist tradition in ways that liberate themselves and others. Collectively we can weave subtle detail and luster into the fabric of our Buddhist narrative and herald the many ways Buddhists, past and present, respond to suffering and seek liberation. The creative expedient of embodied storytelling enables us to hear the voices of women who paved the way for our presence here today and connect to the truth of their sometimes playfully serious wisdom insights. In so doing, we deepen the pool of wise teachers to guide us and reveal their liberating strategies.

I welcome each of you to join me in being our own best Dharma friends and teachers, expanding our sphere to help us create a community that cultivates healing relationships and creates spaces that are refuges of peace.

May we move together as Dharma friends, propelling a vision of liberation to awaken our muddy world with lotus blossoms that emit the fragrance of wisdom and open the heart of compassion.

EPILOGUE

Homage to Our Buddhist Mothers

(TWENTY-FIRST CENTURY, C.E., BERKELEY, CA, UNITED STATES)

We have explored and imagined how women in a range of cultural and historical contexts liberated Dharma principles from misogynist teachings and Dharma practices from patriarchal frames and restrictions. We have listened to ways contemporary women have wielded Dharma to liberate themselves from real and raw forms of suffering.

For the final narration of this book, I will elicit the interdependent nature of liberation by providing a way to move the story off the page and into our bodies. The dynamic sensory medium of ritual can generate a shared communal and embodied experience across space and time. Ritual can sow seeds for future generations as current women who seek liberation connect to women who quested for liberation in the past. Through ritual, we can be transported into this vast liberative stream. In conversation with others, I was inspired to orchestrate such a ritual to enliven women's experiences of liberation.

I began by reflecting on how women have gathered around tables and altars through the ages to share their wisdom and empower themselves and each other to respond to their lived realities. They needed no permission to do so. Many consciously understood and others intuited that communally creating and staging rituals is a powerful way to embody values and commitments. The towering women who have practiced before us attained spiritual heights:

authoritative teachers, wise leaders, ingenious laywomen, generous donors, compassionate mothers, virtuous daughters, and enlightened masters; their fierce discipline, penetrating insights, daily acts of care, and creative devotion to live Dharma—even when faced with obstacles—bequeath a powerful legacy of illuminating wisdom.

As a scholar of women and Buddhism, I feel a duty to help us see the Buddhist tradition more fully. Along with my books, I created this ritual to help free us from the ignorance that distorts our understanding of the capacities and activities of Buddhist women. Since most Buddhist women today are unfamiliar with the range of female ancestors across cultures and times, it is powerful to at least learn and speak the names of eminent women for whom we have records. I have selected seventy-two names from four Buddhist cultures—eighteen names from each—to represent all women. Honoring them affirms and fully claims the Buddhist path as one that is powerfully transformative and liberating for women. Generating awareness of our generational continuity, our matrilineage, through a ritualized chant that heralds the names of our ancestors will help spread knowledge about the accomplishments of past generations that stretch across the vast Buddhist landscape. When we invoke their names, we invoke their energy and viscerally connect with them. That channel opens us up to a deep well of wise strength and visionary vitality.

The ritual, "Homage to Our Buddhist Mothers," brings forth the women whose lives are the foundation of ours.[1] My hope is that each group that offers the ritual will tailor it to their community's cultural and linguistic context, people, concerns, aesthetics, and space. An altar graced by female Buddhist statues sets the visual and spiritual stage. On one occasion of this ritual, the altar was empowered by an exquisite bronze Nepalese Tara, a wooden Guanyin with a dragon at her feet, a brass Mother Maya from Lumbini, an eloquently carved wood Guanyin from Purple Bamboo Grove in China, and an Ittōbori Kannon from Takayama, Japan. Imagine.

HOMAGE TO OUR BUDDHIST MOTHERS RITUAL

> We gather today in homage to our Buddhist mothers. We are grateful for the luminous hearts of all women who gathered wisdom in her bones and contributed to transformation in each cultural milieu as the Dharma traversed India, China, Korea, Japan, and into the West. We honor and thank those who precede us.
>
> Offering candlelight, we illuminate the space with wisdom.
> Offering incense, we release the fragrance of compassion.
> Offering lotus blossoms, we herald each lotus as a
> womb of enlightenment.

Invoking Prajnaparamita, Mother of All Buddhas, puts everyone involved with the ritual into the presence of the source of enlightened being, inviting each person to be ever aware and in touch with the Buddha-nature that animates all life. By proclaiming out loud in each other's presence, we activate our wise and compassionate nature.

> Prajnaparamita, the maternal source of enlightenment is the liberating wisdom that crowns the spiritual quest, personified as a glorious golden goddess installed at the apex of the pantheon as the eternal mother who gives birth to all Buddhas and ever-flowing font of all that Buddhas teach.[2]

Having honored the Wisdom Mother, we invite all women predecessors from all time and space to be present, so we may honor and thank them.[3] (With pure voice and soulful heart, a leader sings a chant in a melody that transports us to their world.)

> Homage to our Indian mothers. Each woman is a lotus blossom. Let us by name thank:

(In an undulating and peaceful refrain, everyone sings the names of each Indian woman.)

Mahaprajapati	Khema	Vijaya
Sujata	Subha	Shishupachala
Patachara	Kisagotami	Soma
Uttama	Chapa	Nanda
Mittakala	Sumana	Sundari
Dhammadina	Abhaya	Punnika

(In succession, we sing homage to our Chinese, Korean, Japanese, and Western mothers, singing their names into a flowing pool of respect and gratitude.)

Homage to our Chinese mothers. Each woman is a lotus blossom. Let us by name thank:

Huixu	Yikui	Tao Shan
Empress Xu	Jizong Xingche	Wang Peihua
Empress Wu	Baochi	Xiaoyun
Miaodao	Zukui	Dawu
Miaozong	Ziyong	Benkong
Xinggang	Daoqian	Longlian

Homage to our Korean mothers. Each woman is a lotus blossom. Let us by name thank:

Pommyong	Chong-sim	Woo Bong Eun
Ukmyeon	Chongyu	Pon'gong
Chinhye	Sonan	Mansong
Queen Sohye	Huiwon	Daehaeng
Myobong	Lady Kim	Pophui
Yi Yesun	Lady Ch'oe	Kim Iryop

Homage to our Japanese mothers. Each woman is a lotus blossom. Let us by name thank:

Egini
Empress Kōmyō
Jōani
Shinmyōni
Myōshinni
Genshuni
Sōkini
Zengoni
Mugai Nyodai
Eshinni
Mizuno Jōrin
Hori Mitsujō
Setouchi Jakuchō
Nogami Senryō
Kuriki Kakujō
Kojima Kendō
Kitō Shunkō
Aoyama Shundō

Homage to our Western mothers. Each woman is a lotus blossom. Let us by name thank:

Flora Eko Courtois
Zenkei Blanche Hartman
Yvonne Rand
Charlotte Joko Beck
Sandra Jishu Angyo Holmes
Jiyu-Kennett
Ruth Denison
Toni Packer
Ayya Khema
Rita Gross
Mitsu Suzuki
Darlene Cohen
Maurine Myo On Stuart
Ruth Fuller Sasaki
Seisho Maylee Scott
Anne Aitken
Jion Susan Postal
bell hooks

Invoking all Buddhist women across time, we breathe life into each of them and illuminate the Jewel-Net of our interdependence. Recognizing ourselves in this precious womb, each a precious pearl of luminous beauty, we pass a pearl one to another as we see each other deeply through the heart. We are each unique, with specific qualities and characteristics. This is our perfection. We are one bright pearl like the natural pearl we offer around the circle before offering it on the altar to Prajnaparamita.

> One bright pearl is able to express Reality without naming it, and we can recognize this pearl as its name. One bright pearl communicates directly through all time; being unexhausted through all the past, it arrives through all the present. While there is a body now and a mind now—they are the bright pearl. That stalk of grass, this tree, is not a stalk of grass, is not a tree; the mountains and rivers of this world are not the mountains and rivers of this world. They are the bright pearl. . . . All the universe is one bright pearl.[4]

Performing and witnessing this ritual infuses us with determination and strength as we are reminded, renewed, and fortified that we are a circle of interdependence committed to being vectors of wisdom and compassion in the world.

> We are profoundly grateful for the nourishment bestowed upon us by a stream of women stretching across millennia and flowing from around the globe. Their presence is palpable in our ever-expanding circle of interdependence, a sacred space where wisdom and compassion bloom.
>
> Homage to Prajnaparamita, mother of all Buddhas, Homage to her daughter, Kannon, and to all Bodhisattvas past, present, and future. May their compassion and wisdom continue to flower in our hearts, bodies, and minds for the benefit and blessing of all beings.
>
> We offer the merit that has been generated for all us beings together to ascend the path of Buddhist awakening.

This ritual is a way to express respect and gratitude for all the women whose thoughts and actions contribute to the Buddhist tradition. I am inspired by the depth of their insights into Dharma, the steadfastness of their discipline and determination, and how their expressions of enlightenment radiate a warm welcome to all beings. Through the ages, women have not developed a doctrine that there are polluted bodies incapable of enlightenment. They tested the third noble truth that there is cessation of suffering, and they found it to be true. In overcoming socially constructed obstacles and dissolving the internally driven poisons of delusion, desire, and aversion, our female forebears shine a light on the supreme potential of women to live Dharma in our muddy world.

We can deepen this stream of liberation by creating stories and rituals that uplift women around us, in our homes, in our communities, in our hearts, in the past, present, and future. What would you include in a liberating story or ritual? Who would you include?

NOTES

EPIGRAPH

1. Wilt Idema and Beata Grant, *The Red Brush: Writing Women of Imperial China*, vol. 231, (Harvard University Asia Center, 2004), 315.

OPENING: WOMBS FOR LIBERATING DHARMA

1. Women were known to visit the lavish gardens of a monastic compound where incense perfumed the air. I drew on materials from Gregory Schopen, "The Buddhist 'Monastery' and the Indian Garden: Aesthetics, Assimilations, and the Siting of Monastic Establishments," *Journal of the American Oriental Society* 126, no. 4 (2006): 487–505, https://www.jstor.org/stable/20064536, and also Gregory Schopen, "The Fragrance of the Buddha, the Scent of Monuments, and the Odor of Images in Early India," *Bulletin de l'École française d'Extrême-Orient*, 101 (2015): 11–30.
2. Miranda Shaw's evidence and analysis of stupas as sites of fecund imagery and evoking a supine pregnant woman's belly inspired me to write this story. For a fuller discussion, please see Miranda Shaw, "Buddhist Practice in South Asia," in *The Oxford Handbook of Buddhist Practice.*, eds. Paula Arai and Kevin Trainor (Oxford University Press, 2022), 22–25.
3. For further discussion, see the following sources: Alison Twells, William Pooley, Matt Houlbrook, and Helen Rogers, "Undisciplined History: Creative Methods and Academic Practice," *History Workshop Journal* 96 (2023): 153–75, https://doi.org/10.1093/hwj/dbad012; William G. Pooley, Matt Houlbrook, Helen Rogers, and Alison Twells, "Creative Histories: Reflections on Research and Practice," *Paper Trails: The Social Lives of Archives and Collections* (UCL Press, 2022), https://ucldigitalpress.co.uk/BOOC/Article/3/120/; William Pooley, "Three Definitions of Creative Histories," Creative Histories of Witchcraft, December 19, 2019,

https://creativewitchcraft.wordpress.com/2019/12/19/three-definitions-of-creative-history/; Sonja Boon, "Creative Histories: Vulnerability, Emotions, and the Undoing of the Self," *Storying the Past: A Blog for Creative Histories and the #Storypast Virtual Reading Group*, October 6, 2017, https://storyingthepast.wordpress.com/2017/10/06/creative-histories-vulnerability-emotions-and-the-undoing-of-the-self-by-sonja-boon/.

4. Shaw, "Buddhist Practice in South Asia," 22.
5. Shaw, "Buddhist Practice in South Asia," 23.
6. Shaw, "Buddhist Practice in South Asia," 23.
7. *Women Living Zen: Japanese Sōtō Buddhist Nuns* (Oxford University Press, 1999).
8. *Bringing Zen Home: The Healing Heart of Japanese Women's Rituals* (University of Hawai'i Press, 2011) and *The Little Book of Zen Healing: Japanese Rituals for Beauty, Harmony, and Love* (Shambhala Publications, 2023).

1. LETTERS OF LOVING GRATITUDE

1. Miranda Shaw, *Buddhist Goddesses of India* (Princeton University Press, 2006), 148.
2. For the stories of prior lives in which Yashodhara and Siddhartha (with different names) were together, see J. J. Jones, trans., *The Mahāvastu*, vol. 1 (Luzac and Company, 1949–1956), 188–203; Andy Rotman, *Divine Stories: Divyavadana*, part 2 (Somerville: Wisdom, 2017), 69; I. B. Horner, trans., *The Minor Anthologies of the Pali Canon*, part 3, *Chronicle of Buddhas (Buddhavaṃsa)* (Pali Text Society), 9–29.

2. PHILOSOPHER QUEEN

1. Diana Paul, trans., *The Sutra of Queen Śrīmālā of the Lion's Roar* (Bukkyo Dendo Kyokai America, 2004), 3–53. For an interpretive discussion of the text, see Diana Paul, "The Concept of Tathāgatagarbha in the *Śrīmālādevī Sūtra*," *Journal of the American Oriental Society* 99, no. 2 (Apr.–Jun., 1979): 191–203.
2. See Paul, *The Sutra of Queen Śrīmālā of the Lion's Roar*, 9, for the incident of a messenger delivering a letter to the queen from her parents; page 11 for the prediction that the queen would become the Buddha of Universal Light; and page 17 for the direct quote "Excellent . . .".

3. FOOD OF LIBERATION

1. Numerous books about Buddhist monastic women have been published in the last few decades, delightfully too many for me to list here.
2. For further information, see my article "Domestic Dharma in Japan" in *The Oxford Encyclopedia of Buddhism*, eds. Richard Payne and Georgios Halkias (Oxford University Press, 2021).
3. For more information on this historical site, see Anuradha Seneviratna, *Ancient Anuradhapura: The Monastic City* (Archeological Survey Department, 1994).
4. In order to bring verity to what Mali might be cooking, my research yielded indigenous foods and traditional recipes of Sri Lanka. S. Mihiranie, J. Jayasinghe, C. Jayasinghe, and J. Wanasundara, "Indigenous and Traditional Foods of Sri Lanka," *Journal of Ethnic Foods* 7, no. 42 (2020), https://doi.org/10.1186/s42779-020-00075-z.
5. In *History of Buddhism in Ceylon: The Anurādhapura Period 3rd Century BC–10th Century AC*, respected Buddhist historian Walpola Rahula provides detailed information about the ways laity supported the monastics in earlier centuries of Sri Lanka's history. (Gunasena & Co., Ltd., 1956), 175–77.
6. The Jetavana stupa was a remarkable architectural accomplishment that towered above the early Sri Lankan landscape, marking Anuradhapura as a major Buddhist center. More details can be found in the following sources: Anuradha Seneviratna, *Ancient Anuradhapura: The Monastic City* (Archeological Survey Department, 1994), 119; Hema Ratnayake, "Jetavana: Stupa and Monastery Complex," in *The Cultural Triangle of Sri Lanka* (UNESCO and Central Cultural Fund, 1993) 64–85.
7. For a map of the monastic compounds around the stupa, see Seneviratna, *Ancient Anuradhapura*, 117.
8. For details of monastic rituals and practices that would have animated daily life at the Jetavana stupa monastic complex, I consulted the following sources: E. W. Adikaram, *Early History of Buddhism in Ceylon: Or "State of Buddhism in Ceylon as Revealed by the Pali Commentaries of the 5th Century A.D.* (Gunasena & Co., Ltd., 1946), 124; R. A. L. H. Gunawardana, *Robe and Plough: Monasticism and Economic Interest in Early Medieval Sri Lanka* (The University of Arizona Press, 1979).

4. LEADING AND BOWING

1. For a detailed explication of this sutra, see Stephanie Balkwill, "The Sūtra on Transforming the Female Form: Unpacking an Early Medieval Chinese Buddhist Text," *Journal of Chinese Religions* 44, no. 2 (2016): 127–48. The "Sūtra on Transforming the Female Form" in Chinese is *Zhuan nüshen jing* 轉女身經 (*Taishō Daizōkyō* no. 564), likely a Chinese-origin text, well-known by Sui (581–618). Texts denouncing women's bodies mostly appeared in meditation manuals aimed at monks to dissolve their lust. In terms of the Buddhist corpus, there are few such texts. Some go over the line and focus on negative characteristics of women's bodies rather than the man's lust. Nancy Schuster's research indicates there were few misogynist authors, though there were a few who wrote vehemently negative things about women. She assessed that most "negative" words about women were intended to support monks who wrestled with lust for women, and they were not declarations about women. Nancy Schuster, "Yoga-Master Dharmamitra and Clerical Misogyny in Fifth-Century Buddhism," *The Tibet Journal* 9, no. 4 (Winter 1984): 41–42.
2. An account of Empress Wu and her tremendous impact on the Chinese Buddhist tradition, including her time in a nunnery (648–651) are given in an article by Patricia E. Karetzky, "Wu Zetian and Buddhist Art of the Tang Dynasty," *Tang Studies* 20–21 (2002): 113–71. Ganye Temple still stands, though now the city is named Xi-an.
3. For a biography of Empress Wu that chronicles her rise to be a female ruler in a patriarchal society, see N. Harry Rothschild, *Emperor Wu Zhao: China's Only Woman Emperor* (Pearson, 2007). See also Yuen Ting Lee, "Wu Zhao: Ruler of Tang Dynasty China," *Education about Asia* 20, no. 2 (Fall 2015): 14–18, www.asianstudies.org/publications/eaa/archives/wu-zhao-ruler-of-tang-dynasty-china/.
4. N. Harry Rothschild details Wu Zhao's entrance to the nunnery on page 191 of his volume *Emperor Wu Zhao and Her Pantheon of Devis, Divinities, and Dynastic Mothers* (Columbia University Press, 2017). He cites, Wang Shuanghuai and Zhao Wenrun, "Leaving the Palace to Become a Buddhist Nun" (*Chujia dang nigu*), chap. 3 in *Wu Zetian pingzhuan*, 21–24. Also see Forte, "Wu Zhao: A Buddhist Novice in her Youth," appendix C in *Political Propaganda*, 365–68.
5. This is a direct quote from the *Sutra on Transforming the Female Body, Zhuan nüshen jing* 轉女身經 *Taishō Daizōkyō* no. 564.

6. Art historian Patricia E. Karetzky offers descriptions of the sculptures in Luoyang and contextualizes their style and significance and the import of Empress Wu's patronage. See her article "Wu Zetian and Buddhist Art of the Tang Dynasty," *Tang Studies* 20 (2002): 113–71.
7. Empress Wu's ruling approach regarding women is discussed in Rothschild, *Emperor Wu Zhao and Her Pantheon*, 17–18.
8. Empress Wu sponsored several Buddhists who had gone to India, studied at Nalanda University, and returned with Buddhist texts. Among them are Xuanzang (602–664) and Fazang (643–712). She supported their translation efforts. Fazang is renowned for his creative efforts to teach Empress Wu the basic principles of a sutra he translated: the *Huayan Sutra* (Skt. *Avataṃsaka*; J. *Kegon*; Eng. *Flower Garland*).
9. Rothschild offers an informed discussion of how the *Sovereign in the Great Cloud Sutra* affected Empress Wu's rise to power. See *Emperor Wu Zhao and Her Pantheon*, 209–10.
10. Norman Harry Rothschild, "Fazang (Fa-tsang, 643–712 C.E.)," Internet Encyclopedia of Philosophy, https://iep.utm.edu/fazang/.
11. Rothschild quotes from the fourth fascicle of the *Sovereign in the Great Cloud Sutra* in *Emperor Wu Zhao and Her Pantheon*, 222.
12. Rothschild reported this event in *Emperor Wu Zhao and Her Pantheon*, 200.
13. Rothschild, *Emperor Wu Zhao and Her Pantheon*, 214.
14. Rothschild, *Emperor Wu Zhao and Her Pantheon*, 225. The fifty-two-foot statue was completed in 676 with the funds Empress Wu offered.
15. Delu Wang, "Indra's Palace on Mount Meru: A Study on the Design Philosophy of Wu Zetian's Bright Hall," *Religions* 15, no. 12 (2024): 1530, https://doi.org/10.3390/rel15121530. Wang's discussion of the philosophical, cosmological, and structural features of the building makes clear that Empress Wu was a visionary who was intent on establishing her place in history.
16. One of eight *Garudharma*, extra rules imposed on *bhikshuni* (J. *bikuni*) nuns. Though presented by some traditions as rules that were a condition of allowing women to join the Buddhist order of mendicants, compelling historical evidence indicates they were compiled at a much later date. Nonetheless, they have been invoked by monastic orders in several Buddhist communities.
17. All evidence suggests men created the Garudharma, so I am not intimating that nuns are responsible for generating a bowing practice that might be detrimental to monks.

18. Stephanie Balkwill translates into English sections of the sutra, including this quote in her article "The *Sūtra on Transforming the Female Form*: Unpacking an Early Medieval Chinese Buddhist Text," *Journal of Chinese Religions* 44, no. 2 (2016): 127–48. The sutra quoted on page 138 uses "female," for which I substituted "male." Balkwill cites T564 921b01-921c03, a code which refers to this passage in the sutra.
19. Balkwill, "*Sūtra on Transforming*," 142–43.
20. This passage from the *Golden Light Sūtra* (Skt. *Suvarṇaprabhāsa-sūtra;* J. *Konkōmyōkyō* 金光明經) is cited in Lori Meeks, *Hokkeji and the Reemergence of Female Monastic Orders in Premodern Japan* (University of Hawai'i Press, 2010), 258. It is an English translation of a Japanese teacher citing the sutra. The changes to the text are mine. The original text is "May all women [nyonin 女人] be transformed into men [otoko 男]."
21. Wang, "Indra's Palace on Mount Meru," 14.
22. Although not verified, see pages 121–22 of Karetzky's "Wu Zetian and Buddhist Art of the Tang Dynasty" for her analysis of the stylistic features that give credence to the legend that Empress Wu was the model for the face of Vairocana Buddha. Karetzky concludes on page 131 that Empress Wu's patronage of Buddhist art resulted in "unstinting creativity."

5. COMPASSION PERSONIFIED

1. Lori Meeks's extensive study of Hokkeji provides substantive historical information upon which this story is based. For the full historical account, see her scholarly findings in *Hokkeji and the Reemergence of Female Monastic Orders in Premodern Japan* (University of Hawai'i Press, 2010). On page 90 of this volume, Meeks notes the kinds of people who came to Hokkeji.
2. See Meeks, *Hokkeji*, 2 for the history of Hokkeji's financial situation from the early ninth to the thirteenth century.
3. See Meeks, *Hokkeji*, 2 for more details.
4. See Meeks, *Hokkeji*, 43 for the reasons why Tōdaiji and Hokkeji needed repair and notes on the significance of Chōgen's efforts to raise funds for these major restorations. See page 47 for details of the statue repairs.
5. See Meeks, *Hokkeji*, 36. When the capital moved to Heian, Nara temples decreased in importance in terms of state affiliations, so the focus in Nara shifted to the temples' sacred origins to attract people. Hence the Nara pilgrimage arose. Meeks also discusses the pilgrimage route and its significance for Hokkeji on pages 24 and 33.

6. See Meeks, *Hokkeji*, 47 for Meeks's elaboration on the legend that accompanies its main Buddhist statue.
7. See Meeks, *Hokkeji*, 37 for details on this legend. Meeks sites the 1911 *Kenkyū gojunreiki*, 142–43.
8. See Meeks, *Hokkeji*, 41 for an explanation of the significance of the bathhouse and its association with Empress Kōmyō.
9. See Meeks, *Hokkeji*, 65 for more information on Jizen.
10. See Meeks, *Hokkeji*, 158 for more information.
11. By 1280 Hokkeji was a large-scale training ground for Ritsu-school nuns whose numbers swelled into the hundreds. See Meeks, *Hokkeji*, 54.
12. See Meeks, *Hokkeji*, 223 for a more thorough explanation of the scriptures the nuns of Hokkeji chanted and the different languages of the chants.
13. The philosophical text they chanted in the Midday service was "Thirty Verses on the *Vijñapati-mātra Treatise* [(*Yuishiki*) *Sanjū* (*ron*) *ju*, Chns. *Wishisanshilunsong*, T. no. 1586; in Chinese]. See Meeks, *Hokkeji*, 218.
14. Had my fictive figure, Chikako, needed refuge from her abusive husband forty years later, she would have had the option to go to a Rinzai Zen nuns' temple, Tōkeiji, in the then capital city of Kamakura (1185–1330). In 1285, it was established in Kamakura by founding abbess Kakusanni and Hōjō Sadatoki. They were, respectively, the wife and daughter of the deceased feudal regent of the Kamakura Shogunate, Hōjō Tokimune (1251–1284). It was common for high-ranking women to become nuns when they were widowed. During that period, men could divorce their wives, but women could not divorce their husbands. The nunnery opened its doors to become a refuge for women seeking divorce, often escaping abusive relationships. For six hundred years, until the law changed, this nuns' temple was a sanctuary for women. It is popularly known by its nickname, Enkiri-dera, temple for cutting connections. Today the nuns permit women and men to respectfully enter the temple grounds, worship at the altar, and enjoy the seasons in the gardens.
15. It was common for aristocratic women to go on pilgrimage to Hokkeji.
16. Aristocratic women and wandering nuns were welcome to stay at Hokkeji for retreats. See Meeks, *Hokkeji*, 83.
17. The nuns of Hokkeji did evening zazen. See Meeks, *Hokkeji*, 219.
18. See Meeks, *Hokkeji*, 219 for more information on the midday service.
19. The *Kannongyō* is the twenty-fifth chapter of the *Lotus Sutra*.
20. Also known as *Daihishindarāni* 大悲心陀羅尼. It is a common chant among Japanese Buddhists. It is often uttered as an expression of gratitude for compassionate support, especially in times of poignant need.

21. Meeks discusses the different levels of ordination in *Hokkeji*, 163–65.
22. See Meeks, *Hokkeji*, 177.
23. NAMU SHAKAMUNI BUTSU means "Take refuge in Shakyamuni Buddha." It is a common chant among Japanese Buddhists. It is often uttered as an expression of gratitude for compassionate support, especially in times of poignant need.
24. On pages 72–76 of *Hokkeji*, Meeks discusses how women of this period would sometimes prefer to have a scroll of *Fugen Raigo* (*Descent of Samantabhadra*) (as opposed to the more common practice of *Amida Raigo*) when they were engaging in their death preparatory ritual, because Fugen resided in Tushita Heaven, a heaven in which women were welcome. *Hokkeji* places the *Fugen Raigo* scroll in a small room, suggesting it was used for private death rituals. In her article "Mothers of the Buddhas: The Sutra on Transforming Women into Buddhas (Bussetsu Tennyo Jōbutsu Kyō)," *Monumenta Nipponica* 71, no. 2 (2016): 263–93, Heather Blair discusses that the teachings of rebirth in Amida's Pure Land were ambiguous about whether women's bodies were accepted in her article.

6. SUTRAS ON SEX TRANSFORMATION

1. For a detailed study of these letters, see James Dobbins, *Letters of the Nun Eshinni: Images of Pure Land Buddhism in Medieval Japan* (University of Hawai'i Press, 2004).
2. Stephanie Balkwill, "Why Does a Woman Need to Become a Man in Order to Become a Buddha?: Past Investigations, New Leads," *Religion Compass* 12, no. 8 (2018).
3. Dobbins, *Letters of the Nun Eshinni*, 40.
4. "Jizoku fujin no ninmu" *Kyōkai Ichiran* 792 (December 15, 1932): 2.
5. Hisao Inagaki, trans., "The Larger Sutra on Amitāyus," in *The Three Pure Land Sutras* (Bukkyō Dendō Kyōkai, 2003), 16.
6. Inagaki, "The Larger Sutra on Amitāyus," 14.
7. Leon Hurvitz, trans., *Scripture of the Lotus Blossom of the Fine Dharma* (Columbia University Press, 1976), 199–201.
8. Hurvitz, *Scripture of the Lotus Blossom*, 58–61. In Japanese, the expedient means of lying is the widely known phrase "uso mo hōben."
9. Hurvitz, *Scripture of the Lotus Blossom*, 201.
10. Robert Thurman, *The Holy Teaching of Vimalakirti: A Mahayana Scripture* (Penn State University Press 1990), 56–63.

11. Thurman, *The Holy Teaching of Vimalakirti*, 61.
12. Thurman, *The Holy Teaching of Vimalakirti*, 62.
13. Heather Blair, "Mothers of the Buddhas: The Sutra on Transforming Women into Buddha," *Monumenta Nipponica* 71, no. 2 (2016): 263–93.
14. Blair, "Mothers," 263. For two copies of the sutra known to be extant, see *Bussetsu tennyo jōbutsu kyō*, Tokyo National Museum and *Bussetsu tennyo jōbutsu kyō*, Historiographical Institute.
15. At an annual meeting of the American Academy of Religion in the early 1990s, in a room with at least two hundred Buddhist scholars, Vajrayana Buddhist scholar and author of *Passionate Enlightenment* Miranda Shaw responded to a critique of her assertion that there are female Buddhas by citing the need for a Buddha to have a "sheathed lingam." There was utter silence when she observed that "sheathed lingam" can also be interpreted as an accurate description of female anatomy.

7. LIBERATING HAIR

1. Carolyn Wargula, "Embodied Objects: Chūjōhime's Hair Embroideries and the Transformation of the Female Body in Premodern Japan," *Religions* 12, no. 773 (2021): 13. Wargula cites Ethan Claude Lindsay, "Pilgrimage to the Sacred Traces of Kôyasan: Place and Devotion in late Heian Japan" (PhD dissertation, Princeton University, 2012), 161, http://arks.princeton.edu/ark:/88435/dsp019c67wm85n.
2. Consult the following sources for more information: Wargula, "Embodied Objects;" Yuhang Li, "Embroidering Guanyin: Constructions of the Divine through Hair," *East Asian Science, Technology, and Medicine* no. 36 (2012), 131–66; Elizabeth ten Grotenhuis, "Bodily Gift and Spiritual Pledge: Human Hair in Japanese Buddhist Embroideries," *Orientations* 35, no. 1 (January/February 2004): 31–35; and Yuhang Li, *Becoming Guanyin: Artistic Devotion of Buddhist Women in Late Imperial China* (Columbia University Press, 2020). In Li's chapter, "Embroidering Guanyin with Hair: Efficacious Pain and Skill" (*Becoming Guanyin*, pp. 7–141), she details the Chinese devotional practice of hair embroidery in the Ming dynasty (1368–1644). The practice was done earlier in both China and Japan, but this chapter offers details of the practice that were likely similar to those settings.
3. Some women even split their hairs to make finer threads, and records indicate some even went blind due to the extreme strain on the eyes.

4. Zenrinji (Temple in a Calm Grove) is the name Emperor Seiwa gave the Shingon sect temple in 863. The temple became a Jodo sect temple in 1224. The founder of the Jodo sect, Honen (1133–1212), was posthumously designated as the eleventh priest of the temple. The temple came to be commonly referred to as Eikan-dō, in memory of a Jodo priest, Eikan, who dedicated temple activity to aid the poor.
5. Stone explains a ritual for the dying that involves five colored cords on page 148 in her volume, *Right Thoughts at the Last Moment: Buddhism and Deathbed Practices in Early Medieval Japan* (University of Hawaiʻi, 2016).
6. On page 152 of *Right Thoughts*, Stone discusses the role and meaning of this scroll painting for death rituals.
7. Japan adopted the Chinese method of time, which designates one of the twelve animals of the zodiac for each two-hour interval. The time of the boar is between 9 and 11 p.m.
8. The Degenerate Age of the Dharma is the final era of time that begins with the Buddha of an era. Each Buddha era unfolds in three phases: True Dharma, Semblance Dharma, and Degenerate Dharma.
9. Elizabeth ten Grotenhuis discusses her research on the Buddhist practice of hair embroidery in the following publications: "Bodily Gift and Spiritual Pledge," 31, where she highlights the significance of Amida's curls being made of human hair, and "Collapsing the Distinction between Buddha and Believer: Human Hair in Japanese Esotericizing Embroideries," in *Esoteric Buddhism and the Tantras in East Asia*, eds. Charles Orzech and Richard Payne (Brill, 2011), 884.
10. Yuhang Li's research discusses how hair embroidery in Japan was part of funerary practices, notably as part of belief in rebirth in the Pure Land. See *Becoming Guanyin*, 118.
11. For more scholarly research on the use of hair to embroider Amida and memorialize the deceased, see page 4 of Carolyn Wargula's article "Embodied Objects" and page 34 of Elizabeth ten Grotenhuis's article "Bodily Gift and Spiritual Pledge."
12. Su Shi (1037–1101) wrote a poem that captures some of the deep qualities of hair embroidery practice of Kannon: *Dongpo quangji*, vol. 1108 of *Yingyin wenyuange siku quanshu* (Taiwan shangwu yingushuguan, 1983–1986), 1108ce, 524. Cited in Yuhang Li, *Becoming Guanyin*, 112. The translation is by Beata Grant and Paula Arai.
13. "Namu Kannon Riki" ([Taking] Refuge in the power of Kannon) is a chant from chapter 25 of the *Lotus Sutra*.

14. For a fulsome discussion of the ritual practice of embroidering with hair as a grieving ritual, see Grotenhuis, "Collapsing the Distinction between Buddha and Believer," 876–92.

8. CHAN MOUNTAIN SUTRA

1. Beata Grant has published numerous books that translate Chan nuns' poetry. She also provides sociohistorical contextualization for the span of time periods. I draw heavily on her scholarship, both through her publications and personal correspondence.
2. Wilt Idema and Beata Grant, *The Red Brush: Writing Women of Imperial China*, vol. 231 (Harvard University Asia Center, 2004), 310.
3. For more context in which the sutra is revealed to Empress Xu, see Idema and Grant, *The Red Brush*, 304.
4. For more context regarding the title of the sutra, see Idema and Grant, *The Red Brush*, 310.
5. For a description of chapter two, see Idema and Grant, *The Red Brush*, 319.
6. Idema and Grant, *The Red Brush*, 318.
7. For more details about these writings, see Idema and Grant, *The Red Brush*, 307.
8. For more details regarding the context for giving Empress Xu this title, see Idema and Grant, *The Red Brush*, 307.
9. Beata Grant offers detailed information about Jizong on page 119 of her volume *Eminent Nuns: Women Chan Masters of Seventeenth-Century China* (University of Hawai'i Press, 2009). On page 23 of the introduction to her book on Jizong Xingche's poetry, *An Anthology of Poetry by Buddhist Nuns of Late Imperial China* (Oxford University Press, 2023), Grant gives an overview of Jizong Xingche's history, which indicates that she was an abbess at a nunnery in Suzhou called Huideng. This was the inspiration that anchored my story in Suzhou.
10. Grant discusses this significant historical text for Chan nuns on pages 128–29 of *Eminent Nuns*. For more nuns' poetry, see Grant, *An Anthology of Poetry*. For the poetry of Jizong Xingche specifically, see pages 242–87 in that volume. For more information about Chinese Chan nuns and their poetry specifically, see Beata Grant, *Daughters of Emptiness: Poems of Chinese Buddhist Nuns* (Wisdom Publications, 2003).
11. For more details about the significance of Jizong's discipline, see page 23 of Grant's *Eminent Nuns*.

12. See Grant, *Eminent Nuns*, 119 for more information.
13. According to Tang dynasty Chan Master Linji, these are the three requisites for enlightenment. See Grant, *Anthology of Poetry*, 279n367.
14. Grant discusses this sermon in "Writing Oneself into the Tradition: Spiritual Autobiographies by Female Chan Buddhist Masters," in *Gendering Chinese Religion: Subject, Identity, and Body*, eds. Jia Jinhua, Xiaofei Kang, and Ping Yao (State University of New York Press, 2014), 47–70.
15. Grant cites Jizong's autobiography on page 56 of "Writing Oneself into the Tradition."
16. On page 57 of "Writing Oneself into the Tradition," Grant details Jizong's description of her breakthrough as written in her autobiography.
17. Grant, "Writing Oneself into the Tradition," 66.
18. Earlier in her life as a nun, Jizong had wanted to leave the mountain to follow her teacher, but he wanted her to stay on the mountain. Upon the sudden death of her teacher, she was appointed the one to ensure his remains were cared for by building a relic stupa and compiling his *Discourse Records*. After leaving the mountain to teach in several places, she returned to this mountain toward the end of her life to write poetry in the tranquility and beauty of the place. For more details, see Grant, *Eminent Nuns*, 114.
19. Grant, *An Anthology of Poetry*, 245.
20. Grant, *Eminent Nuns*, 127. Grant cites, "Nanyue shanju zayong," *Jizong Che chanshi yulu*, J. 28:462a–b.
21. Grant, *Eminent Nuns*, 124. Grant cites, "Zeng Yizhen daoren," *Jizong Che chanshi yulu*, J. 28:464b–c.
22. Grant, *Eminent Nuns*, 115. For this information, Grant cites, "Ji Hengyang Liushi xiongdi," *Jizong Che chanshi yulu*, J. 28:469a.
23. Another of the eight Garudharma, or extra rules imposed on bhikshuni nuns.
24. In Chinese this practice is known as *biguan*.

9. EMBODIED EXPERIENCE

1. There are multiple translations of the title of the sutra, *Ketsubonkyō*, including blood pool, bowl, bath, pond, and menstruation. I am translating it as *Blood Pond Sutra*.
2. For more details see Lori Meeks, "Women and Buddhism in East Asian History: The Case of the Blood Bowl Sutra, Part I: China," *Religion Compass* 14, no. 4 (2020): e12336, https://doi.org/10.1111/rec3.12336; and Lori

Meeks, "Women and Buddhism in East Asian History: The Case of the Blood Bowl Sutra, Part II: Japan," *Religion Compass* 14, no. 4 (2020): e12335, https://doi.org/10.1111/rec3.12335.

3. Meeks, "Women and Buddhism in East Asian History, Part I," 10–11. Meeks cites Jessey Choo, "Historicized Ritual and Ritualized History—Women's Lifecycle in Late Medieval China (600–1000 AD)" (PhD dissertation, Princeton University, 2009), especially chapter 3 and the conclusion.
4. Meeks, "Blood Bowl Sutra, Part II," 4.
5. On page 6 of "Blood Bowl Sutra, Part II," Meeks cites Nei, "Kumano Bikuni no Rikai," in Nei Kiyoshi and Yamamoto Shigeo, *Kumano Bikuni wo Etoku* (Hōzōkan, 2007), 396.
6. Meeks, "Blood Bowl Sutra, Part II," 4. Meeks cites Nei, "Kumano Bikuni no Rikai," in Nei and Yamamoto, *Kumano Bikuni*, 426.
7. Meeks, "Blood Bowl Sutra, Part II," 2. For more in-depth information and context for Mt. Tateyama and activities related to the *Blood Pond Sutra*, see C. Hirasawa, *Hell-bent for Heaven in Tateyama Mandara: Painting and Religious Practice at a Japanese Mountain* (Brill, 2013).
8. Regarding the Tateyama Mandala, Meeks cites Numa, Kenryō, "Tateyama Shinkō to Tateyama Mandara" [Belief in Tateyama and the Tateyama Mandala] *Bukkyō Geijutsu*, 68, 1976.
9. Takemi Momoko, "*Menstruation Sutra* Belief in Japan," *Japanese Journal of Religious Studies* 10, no. 2–3 (1983): 240.
10. For more information about the amulet practices, see Meeks, "Blood Bowl Sutra, Part II," 6. Meeks cites Nei, "Kumano Bikuni no Rikai," in Nei and Yamamoto, *Kumano Bikuni*, 396. See also Hank Glassman, "At the Crossroads of Birth and Death: The Blood-Pool Hell and Postmortem Fetal Extraction," in *Death and the Afterlife in Japanese Buddhism*, eds. Jacqueline Stone and Mariko Namba Walter (University of Hawai'i Press, 2008), 175–206.
11. Takemi, "*Menstruation Sutra*," 242–43.
12. For more information about this revived rite, see Irit Averbuch, "Discourses of the Reappearing: The Reenactment of the 'Cloth-Bridge Consecration Rite' at Mt. Tateyama," *Japanese Journal of Religious Studies* 38, no. 1 (2011): 1–54.
13. These details are documented by Averbuch on page 7 of her article "Discourses of the Reappearing."
14. This aspect of the ritual practice is documented in Meeks, "Blood Bowl Sutra, Part II," 8.

15. Takemi, "*Menstruation Sutra*," 240.
16. On page 10 of her article, Meeks discusses women's groups that met on the nineteenth day of the month. She draws on the scholarship of Nakagami, Kei'ichi, "Jūkuya nenbutsu-tō genryū kō," *Nihon no sekibutsu* 54 (1990): 20–30.
17. Nyoirin Kannon is the specific form of Kannon known to support women, especially with regard to birthing matters. See Meeks, "Blood Bath Sutra, Part II," 12.
18. For more information about these women, see Barbara Ruch, "Woman to Woman: Kumano Bikuni Proselytizers in Medieval and Early Modern Japan," in *Engendering Faith: Women and Buddhism in Premodern Japan*, ed. Barbara Ruch (Center for Japanese Studies, The University of Michigan, 2002), 574–75.
19. Meeks documents the existence of such a pond in "Blood Bowl Sutra, Part II," 7.
20. On pages 10 and 11of "Blood Bowl Sutra, Part II," Meeks details the kinds of concerns and practices of women who gathered in the Nineteenth Night groups. She cites Kobanawa, "Jūkuya-tō," in *Nihon sekibutsu jiten*, 2nd ed., ed. Koshin konwa kai (Yuzankaku, 1980), 171–74.
21. I'm paraphrasing the end of the *Blood Pond Sutra.* Takemi, "*Menstruation Sutra*," 232.
22. On page 4 of "Blood Bowl Sutra, Part II," Meeks explains the historically documented activity of women who went around Japan explicating teachings and offering amulets for a donation.
23. During this period, infant mortality and mothers dying in childbirth were high. In addition, data suggests an estimated 40 percent of babies died through infanticide. See Meeks, "Blood Bowl Sutra, Part II," 11–12. She cites F. Drixler, *Mabiki: Infanticide and Population Growth in Eastern Japan, 1660–1950* (University of California, 2013), 2, 18, 57–73, 109–25.
24. A similar ritual is still being held at Mt. Osorezan. For more details, see Takemi, "*Menstruation Sutra*," 241.
25. This is a quote from the *Blood Pond Sutra* cited in Takemi, "*Menstruation Sutra*," 232. I slightly amended the translation, changing "Pool" to "Pond."
26. This ritual practice is detailed in the *Blood Pond Sutra* itself, which Takemi discusses in "*Menstruation Sutra*," 240.
27. Takemi quotes the *Blood Pond Sutra* in "*Menstruation Sutra*," 229–46.
28. Depicting Tora-san believing women would not be condemned to a Blood

Pond Hell draws on the findings about popular beliefs in the research published in a book by Gorai Shigeru, *Gangōji Gokurakubō chīsei shomin shinkō shiryō no kenkyū* (Research on the materials contained at the Gokurakubō of Gangōji related to popular belief during the medieval period) (Tokyo: Hōzō-kan, 1964), 201.

29. The belief that it was desirable to be reborn in the Pure Land was pervasive in Japan. Takemi, "*Menstruation Sutra*," 242.
30. Takemi details this part of the amulet ritual on page 243 of "*Menstruation Sutra*."

10. EARTHQUAKE AND WAR

1. This is notably so in Japanese culture, where "religion" is not an indigenous concept. Many cultures and languages around the world did not have a word for religion until Western influences were extended in the nineteenth century. Even when a word was created to convey the concept in many languages, the cultures did not integrate the concept into their view of the world. For a thorough discussion of the sociohistorical development of the concept of religion, see Wilfred Cantwell Smith, *The Meaning and End of Religion* (Fortress Press, 1991).
2. For a full discussion of Personal Buddhas see Paula Arai, "Personal Buddhas: Living with Loss and Grief" in *Bringing Zen Home* (University of Hawai'i Press, 2011), 65–107.
3. Renamed Waseda University in 1902.
4. *Tendon* is tempura on top of a bowl of rice with a savory sauce. The restaurant has been in business since it opened in 1887. It's located at 1-38-10 Asakusa, Taito-ku, Tokyo, Japan.
5. A thrilling modern building known as "Cloud Surpassing Pavilion" that energized the Tokyo cityscape.
6. *Nanakorobi, yaoki* is an aphorism associated with Bodhidharma, the recognized founder of Zen Buddhism.
7. This is a phrase of gratitude that means "I humbly and gratefully receive this feast."
8. To lend historical accuracy to the story, I borrowed this date, as well as the date of return, from the actual dates of Iwasaki Tsuneo, a Japanese man who served in World War II. See Paula Arai, *Painting Enlightenment: Healing Visions of the Heart Sutra; The Buddhist Art of Iwasaki Tsuneo* (Shambhala Publications, 2019).

9. This island, now part of Papua New Guinea, is the location to which Iwasaki Tsuneo (see previous note) was actually deployed.
10. Due to a change in weather, the military target was abandoned, and the US military decided to go up the Sumida River where the skies were clear and drop their bombs in an area dense with a civilian population. For more information, see Headquarters XXI Bomber Command, APO 234, "Tactical Mission Report," no. 39, February 25, 1945, pp. 1–7. "In all 453.7 tons of incendiary and general-purpose bombs were dropped on the urban area of Tokyo, destroying approximately 28,000,000 square feet" (p. 5). "Enemy Air Opposition: There were no enemy fighter attacks on this mission" (p. 6). "The major portion of the damage inflicted was in the densely populated section of the city between the northeast corner of the Imperial Palace area and the west bank of the Sumida River" (p. 7). Report signed by Curtis E. Lemay, Major General, USA Document marked "Secret."
11. The *engawa* is an architectural feature of traditional Japanese homes. It is a low wooden veranda that sometimes runs around the perimeter of the house or, at least, along the garden-facing section of the house. It creates a liminal space between the inside and outside of the house. Sitting on the edge of the engawa is an inviting place for people to relax and share casual and intimate conversations.

PART TWO

1. Due to the small scope of the stories of living women in the United States that I offer in this book, they provide only a slim sliver of the perspectives and experiences of Buddhist women. I am grateful for the books and stories that help paint a more detailed picture of our collective landscape. There is so much wisdom to be shared about how women from diverse perspectives wield Dharma in liberating ways, including the following: Chenxing Han, *Be the Refuge: Raising the Voices of Asian American Buddhists* (North Atlantic Books, 2021); Zenju Earthlyn Manuel, *The Way of Tenderness: Awakening Through Race, Sexuality, and Gender* (Wisdom Publications, 2015); Jan Willis, *Dreaming Me: Black, Baptist, and Buddhist; One Woman's Spiritual Journey* (Wisdom Publications, 2008); Toni Pressley-Sanon, *Lifting as they Climb: Black Women Buddhists & Collective Liberation* (Shambhala Publications, 2024); Rima Vesley-Flad, *Black Buddhists and the Black Radical Tradition: The Practice of Stillness in the Movement for Liberation* (New York University Press, 2022).

12. BUDDHA WAS ASLEEP IN OUR HOME

1. An unborn fetus.
2. Jizō Bodhisattva statues abound on street-side shrines and temple grounds throughout Japan, for Jizō is beloved among Bodhisattvas for his focus on caring for children, whether unborn, born, or deceased. Often people, mostly women, will make red bibs to offer to Jizō. Toys are commonly offered to Jizō, intended for the children in his care. Jizō also protects travelers, both in this world and those moving through the six realms of existence delineated by Buddhist cosmology.
3. The poem was edited for length.

15. RIDING WAVES OF GRIEF AND LOVE

1. Excerpt of "Please Call Me by My True Names" by Thich Nhat Hanh in *Being Peace* (Parallax Press, 1987), 67.

16. RITUALS FOR LIVING AND DYING

1. This executive order resulted in the incarceration of approximately 120,000 people of Japanese descent, including US citizens. See www.archives.gov/milestone-documents/executive-order-9066.
2. *Shichi-go-san* literally translates to "seven-five-three."

EPILOGUE

1. People, mostly women, gathered on January 24, 2024, in Berkeley, California, to participate in the ritual "Homage to Our Buddhist Mothers." It was sponsored by the Lenz Foundation and the Soto Zen Buddhist Association to launch their year of "Celebrating the Voices of Women in Buddhism" and was held at the Institute of Buddhist Studies (https://www.szba.org/cvwb2024). Others have also offered this ritual. Other Buddhist sanghas have also developed rituals to honor female ancestors.
2. Miranda Shaw, *Passionate Enlightenment: Women in Tantric Buddhism*, Princeton Classics (University of Princeton Press, 2022), xi–xii.
3. The *Therigatha* provided a rich resource for names of women who were enlightened during the lifetime of the Buddha. They recorded their realizations in verse. There are numerous translations and versions of this

historically important anthology of women's enlightenment songs: Susan Murcott, trans. *First Buddhist Women: Poems and Stories of Awakening*, 2nd ed. (Parallax Press, 2002); Charles Hallisey, *Poems of the First Buddhist Women: A Translation of the Therigatha* (Harvard University Press, 2021); Vanessa R. Sasson, *The Gathering: A Story of the First Buddhist Women* (Equinox Publishing, 2023).

4. Dogen, "Ikka no Myōju, One Bright Pearl," in *Shōbōgenzō: The True Dharma-Eye Treasury*, vol. 1 (Taishō Volume 82, Number 2582), trans. Gudo Wafu Nishijima and Chodo Cross (Bukkyō Dendō Kyōkai Numata Center for Buddhist Translation and Research, 2007), 49–53.

ABOUT THE AUTHOR

Paula Arai holds a PhD in Buddhist Studies from Harvard University and is the first Eshinni and Kakushinni Professor of Women and Buddhist Studies chair at the Institute of Buddhist Studies in Berkeley, California. She also received Zen training at the Aichi Senmon Nisōdō nunnery in Nagoya, Japan, under the tutelage of Aoyama Shundō Rōshi. Throughout her career, she has been generously supported in her pursuits by Fulbright, the American Council of Learned Societies, the Mellon Foundation, the Reischauer Institute of Japanese Studies at Harvard University, and the Frederick P. Lenz Foundation for American Buddhism.

Steeped in ethnographic research, Paula takes an embodied approach to her work and finds poetic immersive storytelling a potent medium for conveying the experiences of the transformative healing she researches. An active public speaker, she also leads workshops on healing rituals. In addition to this work, she has curated exhibits of *Heart Sutra* paintings by Iwasaki Tsuneo, a Japanese scientist and artist, at a number of venues around the United States, including the Morikami Museum, Crow Museum of Asian Art, Peeler Art Center, and Louisiana State University Museum of Art.

Paula enjoys walking in nature with her dog and husband, playing the violin and *taiko*, engaging in thought-provoking discussion with her son, and playing games, especially Pictionary and Bananagrams. Her website is Zenhealing.org.

BOOKS BY PAULA ARAI

Bringing Zen Home:
The Healing Heart of Japanese Women's Rituals
(University of Hawai'i Press)

The Little Book of Zen Healing:
Japanese Rituals for Beauty, Harmony, and Love
(Shambhala Publications)

The Oxford Handbook of Buddhist Practice
(Oxford University Press), coeditor

Painting Enlightenment:
Healing Visions of the Heart Sutra—
The Buddhist Art of Iwasaki Tsuneo
(Shambhala Publications)

Women Living Zen:
Japanese Sōtō Buddhist Nuns
(Oxford University Press)